MADISON PARK REMEMBERED

MADISON PARK
REMEMBERED

JANE POWELL THOMAS

FOR
Kayla, Kyle, Cole, Heidi, Will, Sean, and Erin

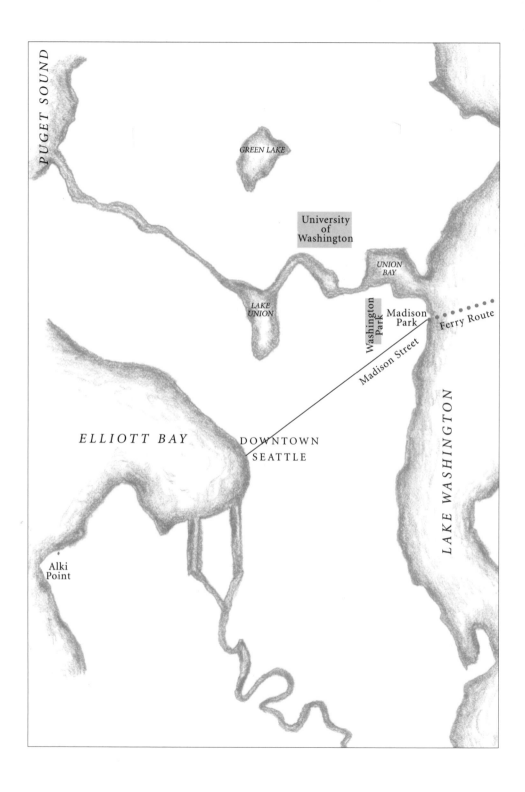

CONTENTS

TIMELINE

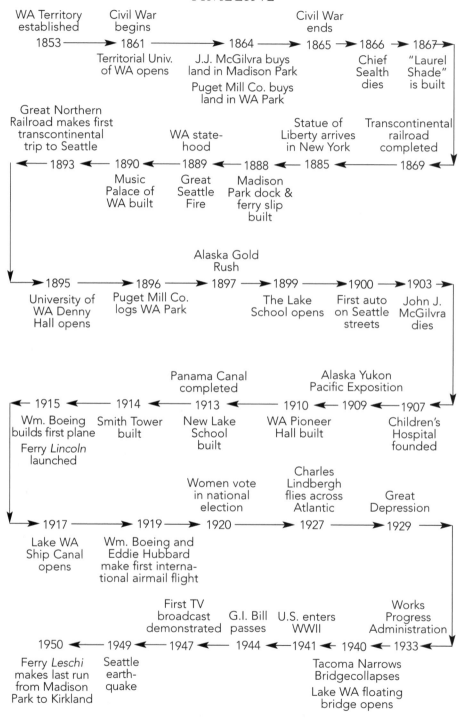

WA Territory established
1853 → Civil War begins 1861 → 1864 → Civil War ends 1865 → 1866 → 1867 →

Territorial Univ. of WA opens

J.J. McGilvra buys land in Madison Park

Puget Mill Co. buys land in WA Park

Chief Sealth dies

"Laurel Shade" is built

Great Northern Railroad makes first transcontinental trip to Seattle

WA state-hood

Statue of Liberty arrives in New York

Transcontinental railroad completed

← 1893 ← 1890 ← 1889 ← 1888 ← 1885 ← 1869 ←

Music Palace of WA built

Great Seattle Fire

Madison Park dock & ferry slip built

Alaska Gold Rush

→ 1895 → 1896 → 1897 → 1899 → 1900 → 1903 →

University of WA Denny Hall opens

Puget Mill Co. logs WA Park

The Lake School opens

First auto on Seattle streets

John J. McGilvra dies

Panama Canal completed

Alaska Yukon Pacific Exposition

← 1915 ← 1914 ← 1913 ← 1910 ← 1909 ← 1907 ←

Wm. Boeing builds first plane

Ferry *Lincoln* launched

Smith Tower built

New Lake School built

WA Pioneer Hall built

Children's Hospital founded

Women vote in national election

Charles Lindbergh flies across Atlantic

Great Depression

→ 1917 → 1919 → 1920 → 1927 → 1929 →

Lake WA Ship Canal opens

Wm. Boeing and Eddie Hubbard make first international airmail flight

First TV broadcast demonstrated

G.I. Bill passes

U.S. enters WWII

Works Progress Administration

1950 ← 1949 ← 1947 ← 1944 ← 1941 ← 1940 ← 1933 ←

Ferry *Leschi* makes last run from Madison Park to Kirkland

Seattle earthquake

Tacoma Narrows Bridge collapses

Lake WA floating bridge opens

PREFACE

Please know that *Madison Park Remembered* is a selective, not an inclusive, history. The intention is to tell a story with reference to world, national, and regional events that contributed to the make-up and fiber of Madison Park.

I chose this format because of my curiosity as to what motivated amazing men and women to settle in this corner of the world, and to what was going on in the rest of the world at the time Madison Park was growing. The reader is asked to trust that the people and events introduced were significant to the development of this community.

I firmly believe that everyone has a story to tell. Those told here are some that are important to me. Family and friends have been most generous with their remembrances, without which this book would not have been possible.

Mt. Rainier was photographed by Ellen M. Banner for *The Seattle Times*.

⮑

ABOUT 13,500 YEARS AGO, the Puget Lobe of the Canadian Ice Sheet retreated to the north. This ice mass, nearly 3,000 feet thick, came to be known as the Vashon Glacier. It left in its path a basin bounded on the east by the Cascade mountain range and on the west by the Olympic range. Among the many fresh and salt waterways carved from this glacial movement were today's Puget Sound and Lake Washington.

The city of Seattle lies at 47° north latitude in the western United States and has a mild, wet maritime climate. Since 1931, the average summer temperature has been recorded as 73°F, and the average temperature for winter months has been 52°F, with an annual snowfall of 10 inches. Situated at nearly the same latitude as Seattle is the Eastern Canada city of Quebec, north of Toronto and Montreal. Canadians there live with an average annual snowfall of 10 feet, offset by hot summers. Several forces of wind and sea contribute to these dramatic differences in the East Coast and West Coast at similar latitudes. The mild winters and comfortable summers in Seattle have been credited to the Japanese current.

On April 10, 1851, John Denny, a 58-year-old volunteer soldier in the War of 1812, politician, and pioneer, left the frontier state of Illinois with other members of the Denny family in four covered wagons headed for Oregon. Accompanying John on this trip, which took 80 days and covered 1,765 miles, were his second wife of only two years, Sarah Latimer Boren Denny, their 6-week-old daughter, Sarah Loretta Denny, and five sons from his first marriage. Oldest of the five, Arthur Armstrong Denny, at age 29, was traveling with his expectant 28-year-old wife, Mary Ann Boren Denny, and their two daughters, Louisa Catherine, age 7, and Margaret Lenora, 4.

David Thomas Denny, at age 19, was 10 years younger than his brother Arthur. Louisa Boren, at 24, accompanied her mother and her older sister, Mary Ann. The Denny party also included the Boren sisters' brother, Carson Boren, age 26, his wife Mary, 20, and their daughter Gertrude, just 1 year old.

Emily Inez Denny, daughter of David and Louisa Boren, who were married early in 1853, wrote that on the fifth of July near the Snake River, the Denny Party came upon Captain John N. Low, his family, and his company of six men and two women.[1] The two groups of emigrants joined forces and traveled the last miles together to Portland. Arthur and David Denny found Portland too populated for their liking, however, so on September 10, David Denny and Captain Low, age 31, started north as an advance party to find the right place for their settlement, walking with two horses that carried their camp provisions.

At the Columbia River, the two men rounded up a few head of cattle belonging to Low and were ferried over to Vancouver, Washington. From there, they followed the old Hudson Bay Company trail to the Cowlitz River; and then along the river's steep, rocky and winding trail to Olympia—a trek of 250 miles. This port of entry to Puget Sound was, in 1851, a town of about twelve one-story framed cabins. There, the two adventurers were joined by Leander Terry, and the three boarded an open boat, the *Captain*, with Captain Robert Fay at the helm, to continue north.

The first white settlers, who are honored today with place names, had arrived just 11 days before the *Captain* and chose claims beyond the boundaries of early Seattle. These men—Luther Collins, Henry

Van Asselt, and Jacob Maple with his son Samuel—built log cabins for their families and cleared the land for farming.

The Denny party spent September 25, 1851, their first night, in Seattle, camped under a cedar tree. This heavily forested land also had Douglas fir and hemlock trees in abundance. Chief Sealth of the Duwamish tribe and his people were camped nearby, and two young Indians agreed to guide the three newcomers by canoe as they explored the area.

On September 28, they recamped at Alki, an Indian name meaning "by and by." Captain Fay convinced Denny and Terry that they would want a log cabin for shelter and protection. Fortunately, David had apprenticed in cabin building before the trip west, but he had only two tools with him to build a home and begin a new life—an ax and a hammer. The men located a "townsite" and named it "New York," a testament to their dreams that before long it would become the metropolis of the Pacific Coast.

John Low returned with Captain Fay to Olympia, then retraced his steps on the Cowlitz trail and south to Portland. Most likely, he was anxious to be reunited with his wife and four children. He carried with him an important penned note for Arthur Denny. It read:

> *Dear Brother,*
> *Come as soon as you can. We have found*
> *a valley that will accommodate one*
> *thousand families. Mr. Low will describe*
> *it to you.*
> *Respectfully,*
> *D. T. Denny*

For weeks, young David Denny was left to his own devices with an unfinished log cabin, the days getting shorter and colder, and primarily in the company of Indians.

Upon receiving his brother's note, Arthur Denny and some of the other families made plans to sail to Puget Sound aboard the 70-foot schooner *Exact*. Some of the roughest waters on the Northwest Coast are found from the Columbia River north up the coast to the entrance of the Strait of Juan de Fuca. Fall of 1851 was no exception.

The five founding families and first settlers arrived at "New York" on November 13, 1851, on a dark and rainy day. The Denny Colony numbered 12 adults and 12 children of the Bell, Boren, Denny, Low, and Terry families. They found David Denny weak from lying ill inside his roofless cabin, but recovering. Before long, they renamed their settlement "New York–Alki," reaffirming their hopes for a promising future.

Soon it became apparent that the shallow waters at this site were not deep enough for navigation or protected enough for anchorage. Therefore, on February 15, 1852, three months after the *Exact* arrived, most of the settlers moved on to the eastern shore of Elliott Bay, which had been sounded with a clothesline and horseshoes.

Arthur Denny later wrote, "After the survey of the harbor, we next examined the land and timber around the Bay, and after three days careful examination we located claims with a view of lumbering, and, ultimately of laying off a town." [2] At that time what we know as Pioneer Square was a small island connected to the shore only at low tide by a sandbar. The Duwamish called this spot "Little Crossing Over Place."

The newcomers staked their donation land claims, and W. N. Bell's cabin was the first one built. Arthur Denny, who was trained as a surveyor, built the second cabin. Soon, Seattle, named for Sealth, chief of the Suquamish and the Duwamish tribes, who would die in 1865 at the age of 80, welcomed its first Euro–American settlers. Those who stayed behind at the original site dropped "New York" from the name and were known from then on as living at Alki.

In March 1853, 11 days after the Territory of Washington was established, Boren, Denny, and Maynard filed the first plats for the "Town of Seattle."

CHAPTER 1

THE EARLY DAYS

ON HIS LAST DAY IN OFFICE, March 1853, President Millard Fillmore established Washington Territory. It was nearly two months later that the residents of Puget Sound learned of their new status.

In June, a U.S. Coast and Geodetic Survey, under the command of Isaac Ingalls Stevens, left Minnesota for the Puget Sound. Sent by President Franklin Pierce, the group was looking for a northern route for a transcontinental railroad. The 35-year-old officer was small in stature, but he was gifted in math and graduated first in his class from

This is the earliest surviving original panoramic view of the city with the Territorial University on the horizon center left, 1865. Photo by E.M. Sammis. Courtesy of University of Washington Libraries, Special Collections. A. Curtis 32137

the United States Military Academy at West Point. His studies of engineering and geography were particularly valuable, enabling him to produce detailed maps and journals during the trip west.

THE FIRST TERRITORIAL GOVERNOR, ISAAC STEVENS

The newly defined Territory—south of the 49th Parallel, north of the Columbia River, east to the Rocky Mountains, and west to the Pacific—called for the appointment of a Territorial Governor. Isaac Stevens was named to that post in 1854, and his title and responsibilities later were extended to include those of Superintendent of Indian Affairs. Stevens worked diligently and successfully to improve postal service and roads, and he secured $5,000 for books for a territorial library. He advocated to the United States Congress for money to finance a university and enlisted the 10-acre donation of land at 4th and University Street from Arthur Denny, Lee Terry, and the Honorable Edward Lander, Chief Justice of the Territory. The Territorial University of Washington opened in Seattle in 1861—the same year that marked the start of the Civil War—with thirty students and one teacher. Preparatory subjects were part of the curriculum for many years.

PIONEER JOHN JAY McGILVRA

In the same year, President Abraham Lincoln appointed John Jay McGilvra to be the first United States Attorney for the Territory of Washington. McGilvra was born in 1827 in Livingston County, New York, into a family with seven children. Of Scotch ancestry, he worked from the age of 12, doing chores for $4.00 a month. When he was 17, he moved with his family to Illinois, where he attended school and worked for his board and room. McGilvra read the law and was admitted to the bar in 1853.

Lincoln and McGilvra practiced law in the same building in Chicago. With a door between their offices, they had a mutually beneficial arrangement in which each looked after the other's clients when one or the other was out of town. The two men developed a mutual respect and became friends.

With his wife of 6 years, Elizabeth Hills McGilvra, he traveled west in 1861, at age 34, to assume his new duties in the Territory. Seattle's population in 1862 numbered only 182, when a significant piece of congressional legislation, The Homestead Act, was passed. After 70 years of controversy over the handling of public lands, fueled by the issue of slavery spreading into the western territories, the War Between the States

John J. McGilvra, ca. 1895. Courtesy of Museum of History and Industry, Seattle. SHS 120

offered a resolution. The secession of the southern states cleared the way for the Act, which stipulated that anyone could file for a quarter-section (160 acres) of free land. The land became the settler's after 5 years if he built a house, dug a well, plowed 10 acres, fenced the land, and actually lived there.

It is no coincidence that Seattle's growth from the Elliott Bay waterfront to the east toward Lake Washington was spurred by this land grant legislation. After traveling throughout the region, studying the development of the West in his capacity as the U.S. Attorney for Washington Territory, McGilvra became convinced that Seattle would become the metropolis of the Territory, despite popular opinion to the contrary.

McGilvra declined reappointment as U.S. Attorney after serving 3 years, tiring of all the travel it required. He turned his attentions to the private practice of law, to his family, which now included two daughters and a son, and to investment in real estate. He purchased 420 acres on the western shore of Lake Washington from the U.S.

government and the Territory, which were interested in raising money for a Territorial University. The Duwamish Indians called this land "Where One Chops." Access to his property required that McGilvra pay $1,500 to have a trail cleared through the forest to Lake Washington. Today we know this trail and property as Madison Street and Madison Park.

John and Elizabeth McGilvra moved into the first home built on the forested shore of Lake Washington. The year was 1867, and the home came to be called "Laurel Shade." This remote and modest white frame house, where the couple raised their three children, was the only home in Madison Park for many years. McGilvra, leading an active political and professional life, used his horse-drawn stage along the newly cleared trail to reach "downtown." Two years later, the Territory incorporated McGilvra's downtown, the city of Seattle. The new city was bounded by today's Galer Street on the north and Hanford Street on the south, and stretched from Elliott Bay east to Lake Washington. At that time, Seattle boasted a population of 1,107.

McGilvra's daughter Caroline, in 1879 at age 22, married a 30-year-old attorney from New York who had been in Seattle four years, Thomas Burke. He became a Probate Court Judge, and then Chief Justice of the Supreme Court of the Territory of Washington. McGilvra's son-in-law and law partner distinguished himself as a community leader in the fields of law, education, and railroads. Both he and Caroline became active in civic and cultural groups.

DEVELOPMENT AROUND LAKE WASHINGTON

Pioneer Ezra Meeker wrote, "Lake Washington, eighteen miles long and averaging about two miles in width, lies immediately East of Seattle. At a light cost this inland navigation can be rendered available for light draft steamers, adding a beautiful water front to the city, should the wants of commerce ever demand so large an area."[1]

The tallest of the mountains to the east of Madison Park and Lake

Washington, and a majestic presence in the Cascades, was first called Tahoma, "the mountain that was God." It was renamed Mt. Rainier in 1792 by Captain George Vancouver of the British Royal Navy. The mountain rises 14,411 feet above sea level and was formed about a million years ago.

For many years, residents east of Lake Washington rowed or sailed to McGilvra's property, then walked up the trail and down into town to conduct business. Soon small independent steamboats carried passengers to the landing and McGilvra offered rides via his horse-drawn stage. McGilvra's dock was the busiest private landing on the Lake for many years, with a scheduled ride downtown in the morning and a return trip to the Lake in the evening.

Eventually the McGilvra family began a development plan for their Lake Washington property "so far from town." McGilvra negotiated with the Madison Street Cable Railway for a line extension from the top of Capitol Hill to the Lake, in exchange for 21 acres of his waterfront property, to be used as picnic grounds, and a $50,000 subsidy for the cable car company. It was further stipulated that the company would build terminal facilities for its railway and develop the park with a pavilion for the mutual economic benefit of the McGilvras and the cable company.

The Madison Park dock and steamer ferry slip were built, and to coordinate with this lakeshore development, the cable car service that McGilvra had negotiated began running from Madison Park to downtown in 1889.

McGilvra's investment in the Madison Street Cable Railway helped bring to reality his vision of a resort and amusement park on Lake Washington, and by 1890 the five-turreted Music Palace of Washington was complete. Built by George K. Beede, it could seat 500 people and there was outdoor seating for hundreds more, drawn to the 21-acre park for concerts, plays, and dances.

For more than 20 years, Dad Wagner's band provided the music— often John Philip Sousa marches. There were canoes for paddling and

The Music Palace of Washington in Madison Park was a popular place to visit at the turn of the century. Courtesy of the Museum of History and Industry, Seattle. 83.10. 6716

a boardwalk for promenading. Olive Baker McDougall recalled in her memoir that the band wore black uniforms with red trim.[2]

Across Madison Street to the north, land was cleared for Seattle's first professional baseball park. Grandstands were built, and Sunday afternoon games were scheduled for the Pacific Northwest Baseball League. For the first game, May 24, 1890, following a customary 6-day work week, as many as 1,200 fans enthusiastically packed the stands. The unnamed Seattle team, called "our boys," played a team from Spokane Falls and won 11–8. Wearing blue and white, the team, which had no mascot, competed with teams from Tacoma, Portland, and Spokane.

THE POPE AND TALBOT COMPANY

In 1853, a party led by Captain William Chaloner Talbot arrived at Port Gamble at the head of Hood Canal. He had sailed from San Francisco in search of a site for a lumber mill. Talbot and Alexander Jackson Pope were from timber families in Maine and had arrived in San Francisco four years earlier, recognizing the business opportunities that growing city offered. The Forty Niners mining for gold in California began looking to the barely populated Pacific Northwest for Douglas fir. Timber was needed for shoring up mining tunnels, as supports for rail tracks, and for buildings in the mining towns.

Accompanying the two men north aboard the small schooner *Julius Pringle* was Cyrus Walker. He initially served the William C. Talbot & Company at Port Gamble as timekeeper, accountant, and general utility man. Once Captain Talbot's mill was sited, he returned to Seattle and Yesler's mill to arrange for the first cargo of lumber to go to San Francisco aboard the *Pringle*.

In 1864, Pope and Talbot bought their first 80-acre tract in Seattle from the government for $100. Pope, together with Frederic Talbot, a brother of William, founded the now dominant lumber company of Puget Sound and soon increased their holdings to more than 200 acres, for what would become Broadmoor. The company's purchases continued and finally included what we know as Washington Park and the Arboretum.

The Pope and Talbot timberlands became the western boundary of John McGilvra's Madison Park real estate holdings. Timber inter-

A major link between the East Coast and Seattle was accomplished on October 25, 1864. With thanks to Samuel B. Morse and Western Union, information could be transmitted by telegraph wire for the first time. No longer did pioneers in the Northwest have to wait days or weeks for a ship or an overland delivery to know what was happening across the country.

ests of Pope and Talbot in Washington State were named the Puget Mill Company in 1874, and Pope and Talbot remained as the San Francisco agents.

Puget Mill Company, which had owned and held the forested property bordering Madison Park for 32 years, began logging in 1896 between 33rd and 37th Avenue North and from Union Bay south to East Valley Street.

THE RAILROADS AND LOGGING—SOL GROUT SIMPSON AND MARK EDWARD REED

While the Civil War continued to result in unprecedented loss of life and property in the East, the U.S. Congress recognized the importance of governing the territories. In 1864, the government granted a charter to build a railroad from Lake Superior to the Pacific Coast. This predecessor of the Northern Pacific Railroad was granted 40 million acres of land, made up of the odd-numbered sections in a belt 40 miles wide on either side of the transcontinental line through the territories.

Railway engineers used the 1853 maps of the first territorial governor, Isaac Stevens, careful to plot a course that would secure the land that was most valuable in timber and minerals. The line was destined to terminate in Portland, Oregon.

Over the years, the Northern Pacific sold or leased the chartered lands. Many of the contracts included "preferential routing" clauses, which stipulated that all commodities produced or manufactured on these lands would be shipped over Northern Pacific rail lines, as long as the Railroad's prices remained competitive.

At last, on April 9, 1865, Robert E. Lee surrendered at the Appomattox Court House. The years of grieving and reconstruction would begin both north and south of the Mason–Dixon Line. For many, going West offered the promise of new beginnings, new opportunities and a new life.

In May 1869, the final and golden spike was driven at desolate

Promontory Point, Utah, completing the first transcontinental railroad to San Francisco. Suddenly a trip that took many months by wagon took only a week or two by rail.

After years of competition between Seattle and her sister port city to the south, in 1873 Tacoma was named as the Puget Sound terminus for the Northern Pacific Railroad. Not until 1887 was the line completed from Portland to Tacoma, bringing transcontinental rail transportation to Tacoma's Commencement Bay. The Pacific Northwest was now linked to the South, the East, and the rest of the country.

According to Robert Ficken, who chronicled the lumber industry in Washington, Sol Grout Simpson was born in Quebec to a New England family, and in 1877, at 34 years of age, moved to Seattle with his new wife, Mary James Macon Garrard, known as "Tollie."[3] A year later, a daughter, Irene Marie, was born. Simpson developed a successful contracting firm, grading city streets. He then demonstrated his skills at grading railroad lines for the coal mines south and east of the city. Moving coal from Newcastle across the isthmus between Union Bay and Portage Bay necessitated that a narrow-gauge railway be built. Between 1872 and 1878, Seattle's principal export was coal, not lumber.

Andrew Price, Jr., wrote that Captain William Renton hired Sol Simpson in 1886 to grade the Blakely Line. "The terminus of the logging railroad, where logs could be dumped into the saltwater for towing to Port Blakely, was seven miles south of what became the town of Shelton."[4] Simpson arrived at the Port Blakely Mill Company "with a crew of experienced road builders and a few horses. A forceful and innovative man, the wiry Simpson quickly impressed his new associates."

By 1890, Simpson had begun buying timberland "apparently with money borrowed from Captain Renton," having resigned from Port Blakely to set up S. G. Simpson and Co. in the western part of Mason County. Five years later Simpson and Alfred Horace Anderson formed the Simpson Logging Company.[5]

Author Ficken reported that Thomas Milburne Reed, with his

wife Elizabeth Finley Reed, both Kentucky-born, moved to the Washington Territory in 1857, when Reed was 32 years old. He came to serve as the Wells Fargo agent for Olympia and was highly regarded by his contemporaries and active in territorial political and social affairs.[6] Nine years later Mark Edward was born, their second son to survive infancy. Tragically, Elizabeth Reed died only four days later from complications of Mark's birth, and he was raised by two successive stepmothers in Olympia. His father's business ventures were only marginally successful.

Mark Reed graduated in 1887 from the California Military Academy in Oakland and returned to Olympia, where for the next couple of years he worked with his father and studied law with attorney James Augustus Haight. Although he did not complete his law studies, he recalled later, "I am thankful for my law training. It helped me out of many a spot. Every young businessman should have some knowledge of the law."[7]

Reed went to work for Simpson Logging Company in 1897, as a foreman at Camp One in Mason County. During this assignment Reed met "Sol Simpson, one of the most important loggers in the state." The next year Reed was brought to Shelton to manage the Lumberman's Mercantile Company, in which Simpson and Anderson owned a major interest. Reed was given more and more responsibility within the company and the industry.

In 1901, at age 34, Reed married Simpson's 23-year-old daughter, Irene Marie, in Seattle. From there they left aboard ship for Nome, Alaska, on their honeymoon. By late summer they were back in Shelton, where Reed gradually assumed day-to-day management of his father-in-law's properties. The Reeds welcomed their first son, Sol Simpson Reed, in 1902. By 1908, there were two more boys, Frank Campbell and William Garrard, to complete the family.

Sol Simpson, in failing health, died in 1906 at age 63 at his daughter's home in Shelton. Mark Reed had been given control of the Simpson Logging Company and its "three hundred employees and five camps producing up to three hundred thousand feet of logs a day."[8] The company's headquarters was moved to Shelton. Shortly thereafter, Reed took out a bank loan to acquire the stock owned by the Port Blakely investors.

THE FIRE OF 1889

The histories of many American cities have recorded disastrous fires from which pioneer citizens not only survived but triumphed. On June 6, 1889, Seattle burned. At 2:45 p.m. in Victor Clairmont's Cabinet Shop in the Pontius Building at Madison and Front Street, several men were working in the basement. Among them was John E. Back, a young immigrant from Sweden. He was in charge of the glue pot, which erupted in flame. The volunteer fire department was hampered in dousing the blaze by warm, dry weather and a low tide. By sunset, the entire business district—29 blocks of wooden structures and 10 brick buildings—was in ruins. With the burning of 64 acres, miraculously there was no loss of human life.

Only 2 weeks later a city ordinance was approved, stipulating that reconstruction must be of brick and stone and the buildings must be situated on wider streets. A new generation of architects was drawn to Seattle to design buildings of four to seven stories, which would meet the new requirements. Very soon 130 new buildings were constructed, among them the predecessor of the Frederick & Nelson department store, destined to be the city's finest for 102 years. During the year after the fire, Seattle's population grew from 25,000 to 43,000. The rapid civic growth was fostered by the national rail connections.

This frontier town in the Northwest drew a population that was mostly male. Single men worked in the timber, fishing, and building trades and spent their earnings and leisure time gambling and frequenting saloons and houses of ill repute. In its first year of post-fire reconstruction, the need for men with professional training in business, politics and urban design grew substantially.

STATEHOOD AND BEYOND

As if emerging from the Great Fire didn't provide enough excitement, on November 11, 1889, President Benjamin Harrison signed the document proclaiming Washington a state. With the arrival of statehood, Washington's constitution mandated that its top priority would be education. President Harrison came to Seattle in May 1891, the second President to visit the city. Although he was in town just 4 hours, his tour included a Yesler Street cable car ride to Lake Washington, a boat ride on the steamer *Kirkland* from Leschi to Madison Park, and a trip downtown on the Madison Street cable car, before speaking to a crowd of 35,000 at the University.

The first President to make an official visit to Seattle was President Rutherford B. Hayes, coming aboard a sailing ship in 1880. By then, Seattle's population had grown to 3,553, twice what it had been the previous decade. Seattle's residents finally outnumbered those of Walla Walla in 1881, and just 2 years later the population of Seattle doubled again.

Families started to spend not just their summers in Madison Park, but they became year-round residents. Families mean children, and children must have a school. In 1891, the Seattle School Board authorized the $9,000 purchase of a city block offered by owner McGilvra, north of Madison Street and bounded on the west by Puget Mill Company property.

With annexations north and west of Seattle in 1891, McGilvra's homestead no longer lay half in and half out of the city limits and Madison Park officially became a neighborhood in Seattle. From Walk V (now East McGilvra Street) south beyond the Firloch Canoe Club, small lots were platted and leased for $15 a month. McGilvra allowed renters to build small summer cottages, or "tent houses," on these lots. Along the Lake, wooden walkways led to houseboats. Twin bandstands went up offshore, on which light operas such as those of Gilbert and Sullivan, were presented.

The Seattle Tennis Club, located at the corner of Minor and

Canoeists paddle at Madison Park, with the offshore bandstands in the background, ca. 1910. Courtesy of Museum of History and Industry, Seattle. 1983. 10. 8642

Madison since 1890, purchased the old, shingled Firloch Canoe Club grounds for $22,500. This relocation on the western shore of Lake Washington provided a long sought-after site to accommodate the Tennis Club's growing membership. In 1919, the Club's president reported on the efforts the City was making to improve the road going by the club grounds—that rough-planked road, framed by fir trees, we know today as McGilvra Boulevard.

In James Warren's history of the Tennis Club, he wrote, "As the years passed, more and more automobiles thumped over the planks. Yet all through the decade, horse-drawn wagons rattled down the street to deliver ice or groceries."[9] Warren also wrote that Caroline McGilvra Burke (Mrs. Thomas) served as president of the Seattle Tennis Club Women's Board between 1920 and 1932.

In his family history, George Powell wrote, "When I was young, none of the kids in our neighborhood belonged to the Tennis Club. When we wanted to go swimming during the summer, we would go straight from our house down towards the Lake and cross McGilvra Boulevard (40th Avenue North) into a patch of woods just south of the Tennis Club. There we would undress and get into our swimsuits (in those days even a boy's swimsuit was something like a leotard, there was nothing like bathing trunks). And then we would make our way down the hill to the water and eventually a few yards north to the beach in front of the Tennis Club and use the Tennis Club's raft. As years went by and we were a little older, we would become members of the Tennis Club and use its facilities in a more straightforward manner."[10]

The last decade of the nineteenth century placed Seattle in the spotlight of the West Coast boom, dictated by topography and by transportation. Authors Jeffrey Ochsner and Dennis Anderson pointed out that the increasing demand for residential construction was almost exclusively in the single-family pattern. Neighborhoods sprang up along the electric and cable car lines that radiated out from the downtown business district.[11]

In 1897, Seattle began a love affair with bicycles that would last for ten years. The Paths Committee of the Queen City Good Roads Club organized a group of volunteers who constructed 25 miles of bicycle paths from Bailey Peninsula at Seward Park north along Lake Washington. The bicycles shared city roads with pedestrians and those in horse-drawn carriages.

JAMES JEROME HILL, THE EMPIRE BUILDER

Although the Northern Pacific Railroad reached Tacoma and its terminus on Puget Sound 30 miles to the south, Seattle was connected only by a trunk line. Until 1887, an inconvenient overnight and a change of trains in Tacoma were necessary before traveling on to Seattle.

Then came a man, who is known as "the Empire Builder." Canadian-born James Jerome Hill lost his father and one of his eyes as a boy. While still in his teens, he moved to St. Paul. He achieved financial success in several ventures, which allowed him to invest privately in building the rail line from St. Paul through Stevens Pass to Everett. Of note is that Hill was represented by attorney Thomas Burke, son-in-law of John McGilvra.

The Great Northern Railroad finally reached Seattle in 1893. At last, not just passengers, but also lumber and salmon, could move overland to the rest of the country. Commerce by sea through the Port of Seattle also expanded at a tremendous rate with shipping trade to Asia.

Just three days into the new century, Hill sold 900,000 acres of Washington state timberlands to Frederick Weyerhaeuser. In one of the largest single-land transfers in U. S. history, this transaction established the timber company that remains the largest in the state.

Both the Great Northern and the Northern Pacific railroads welcomed the opening of the King Street Station in 1906. The 5,146-foot-long railroad tunnel, 110 feet below downtown Seattle, was completed.

In Powell's family history, he wrote, "In all the years I attended McGilvra there was only one African American in the school and he was in my grade. His name was Archie Anderson and he went to work for the NPR. He ended up in charge of the private car of the President of the Northern Pacific Railroad." [12]

Jacqueline Lawson wrote that Anderson was born in Seattle on December 27, 1908, the son of Lucius and Celestie Anderson.[13] He attended Tougaloo State College and married Oralee Coopie of St. Paul. The Andersons had three children—a daughter, Martha Naomi, and two sons, Lucius Archie and Marvin Roger. After a long career with the NPR, Anderson died in 1966.

The Powell family celebrated two weddings in 1925: Sargent Gastman married Grace Charlesworth in June, and in September Achsa Louise married Lochren Donnelly. Donnelly was born in 1897 in St. Paul and graduated from Princeton University. He came to Seattle as assistant to the general manager of the Northwest Improvement Company, the mining arm of Northern Pacific Railroad, with offices in the Smith Tower.

Following their wedding, the Donnellys moved to Montana to another NPR assignment. Five months later, Donnelly became ill with a ruptured appendix. Penicillin was not yet available, and he died in1926. His widow, Achsa, a graduate of Smith College, returned to Seattle to the comfort of her family on 37th Avenue North. Donnelly's father Charles, president of the Northern Pacific Railroad until his death in 1939, also survived him.

ALASKA GOLD

In the 1890s, two primary events led to Seattle's rapid growth. The first was the long-sought arrival of direct transcontinental rail service in 1893. The second came in 1897 with the discovery of gold in Alaska.

Skookum Jim, Dawson Charlie, and George Carmack found the first gold nugget at Rabbit Creek, a tributary of the Klondike River in the Yukon Territory. It was the size of a dime. A year later the steamship *Portland* arrived at Schwabacher's Wharf on Elliott Bay from the Klondike with 68 prospectors aboard. As these men came ashore, they were smiling and straining under the weight of sacks of gold nuggets mined in Alaska. A crowd of 5,000 greeted the ship.

Seattle immediately began a public relations campaign, promoting itself as the starting point for fortune hunters headed north. The railroads could bring adventurers to Seattle, they could purchase supplies at dockside, and steamers could carry the gold-seekers to Skagway or Dyea, from where they would make the extremely difficult journey to Dawson City. From Seattle it was a 3-week trip to the gold fields, and possible to undertake only in the late spring and summer before freezing conditions began.

By law, each Klondike miner had to invest in one ton of supplies, enough to last a year. Paul Dorpat wrote that these supplies might include "yellow corn meal, whole peas dried, lentils, lanterns, lye, summer sausage and sleds,"[14] which then would then be shipped to Alaska. By the spring of 1898, $25 million in goods had been sold in Seattle. Schwabacher Brothers and Company, a hardware retailer established in 1890, earned a reputation as the "Klondike Outfitters."

One of the brothers was Sigmund Schwabacher, who was born in Bavaria in 1841 and came to Washington Territory in 1861. His eldest son, Leopold, was an 8-year-old when the *Portland* docked in Seattle.

By early 1899, the Gold Rush was virtually over, but Seattle entered the twentieth century with a population of 80,671, almost double what it had been in 1890. The pioneer merchants met with a lot more prosperity than did the men and women who endured unbelievable hardship chasing a dream to Alaska.

STEAMBOATS AND FERRIES—JOHN ANDERSON

For many years, McGilvra and other civic leaders campaigned for a canal joining Lake Washington and Puget Sound. Historian Richard Berner wrote, "The canal would also provide a route to float raw timber from east of Lake Washington into Puget Sound; it would also mean that coal would no longer have to be barged, then portaged, from east of the lake to Elliott Bay."[15] In 1884, the same year the Washington Monument was completed by Army engineers in the nation's capital, Seattle took its own significant step and started cutting through the isthmus and building the Lake Washington Ship Canal. A guillotine gate lock was built near the Portage Bay end of the cut and was known as the Montlake log canal locks.

At the insistence of Kirkland residents on the east side of Lake Washington, the King County Port Commission established public ferry service to Madison Park in 1900. The many little steamboats on the lake were too small for wagons and horses and stopped at too many docks. The double-ended ferry offered regular service, although the smaller independent steamers still competed with the county for business along the shoreline.

Captain John L. Anderson founded the Anderson Steamboat Company in 1893, having arrived in the Puget Sound area 5 years earlier with just $20 in his pocket. He worked as a deckhand and before long earned his master's license and bought his own boat, *Winnifred.*

By 1908, Anderson had bought up most of the Mosquito Fleet of independent boats. As a private monopoly on the Lake, his steamers could stop at any dock and keep any schedule. James Warren wrote, "A white flag, hung where it could be seen, signaled these small lake steamers to stand-to for passengers and/or goods often delivered by canoe or rowboat."[16] This was also the year he opened the Anderson Shipyard south of Kirkland.

Anderson built his first side-wheeler ferry, the *Leschi*, in 1913. In addition to passengers, it could also carry automobiles. Two years later, the Anderson Shipyard launched the ferry *Lincoln*. The largest passenger/auto ferry to ever run on the Lake, the *Lincoln* was managed by the King County Port Commission and was a favorite with Madison Park commuters. She was roomy and, more than that, fast and dependable. The *Lincoln* did not miss a scheduled trip in 25 years.

Anderson's expertise at operating a boat business finally earned him the county position of superintendent of ferries—but not before he got in trouble with both the Port Commission and Kirkland. While competing with the county ferry, Anderson's little boats simply showed up at the public dock, picked up passengers, and were under way minutes before the ferry landed. Eventually a resolution was found, and from 1922 to 1935, Anderson's administrative abilities were recognized and appreciated by public and private interests alike.

The last survivor of the steam-powered boats is the *Virginia V*, one of the larger of the fleet. In her early days she served communities on the west side of Vashon Island in Puget Sound.

UNIVERSITY OF WASHINGTON AND JOHN HAVARD POWELL

When Seattle's boundaries were pushed north and west in 1891, the city's size virtually doubled. Edmond S. Meany was elected to the State legislature in 1891 and 1893 and, while there, chaired a committee concerned with the acquisition of land for a new University of Washington campus.[17]

In 1895, many of the city's historical street names were changed to numbers, and that year also saw the first building completed and opened for instruction on the new University of Washington campus. Named Denny Hall, it stood alone surrounded by virgin timber and native undergrowth. The University catalog designated the campus as Grounds and Arboretum.

The Board of Regents at the University issued a statement in 1899 that "in addition to all the other needs of the institution, there could be established here a scientific arboretum." Donald Sherwood, a Seattle Parks Department engineer, became known as the department's historian. He wrote that the Puget Mill Company negotiated to give the City 62 acres of the ravine area of Washington Park in exchange for a $35,000 water main project for its real estate development.[18] The "real estate development" became Broadmoor, and the "ravine" is what we know today as the University of Washington Arboretum.

In 1902, the University of Washington had an enrollment of just over 600 students and named a new president. Thomas Franklin Kane, a Latin professor, assumed office and set about establishing important fishery and forestry links with the region's economy.

That was the year McGilvra gave one of his lakefront lots as the site for the Washington Pioneer Hall. At one point, McGilvra was president of the Washington State Pioneer Association, an association of lineal descendants of the Pioneers of Washington Territory.

Another notable benefactor was Sarah Loretta Denny, daughter of John and Sarah Boren Denny and half-sister of Arthur and David Denny. She was an infant in 1851 when her parents and extended family traveled west from Illinois in a wagon train. Ever mindful of her pioneer heritage and out of devotion to her parents, she left a bequest of $20,000 for building Washington Pioneer Hall to preserve "the history of territorial days through a collection of biographical materials of Pioneer families."[19] Sarah Denny died at age 58. The Hall stands today in Madison Park on the property given 7 years earlier by John McGilvra and is listed in the National Register of Historic Places.

Washington Pioneer Hall was photographed by Arthur Churchill Warner ca. 1915. Courtesy of University of Washington Libraries, Special Collections. Warner 281

Of further note, President Theodore Roosevelt was the third President to visit Seattle. He spoke to 60,000 citizens on the University of Washington campus in 1903.

The university's first football game was played at Husky Stadium on November 7, 1920, with every one of the 30,000 seats taken. The University of Washington invited Dartmouth College for this historic event—and lost 28–7. George Powell remembers going to the game with his family when he was ten years old: "One could follow the trails through the Puget Mill property all the way to what was known as Foster Island, which is near the east end of the Montlake Cut. The cut had not been made in my youth and there was, of course, no Montlake bridge. However, there was a slough running between Lake

Washington and Lake Union so it was usually not possible to cross over to the University grounds. They had put wooden floats in the slough and I can recall members of my family going to that game, walking through the Puget Mill property and over the wooden barges or floats up to the stadium and then going home the same way."[20]

A leader in the development of the University of Washington was John Havard Powell, an attorney from Illinois. The ninth of ten children, he was accustomed to long hours of chores on the family farm, followed by many hours of work studying for a university degree, where he was president of his senior class at the University of Michigan. After reading the law and being admitted to the Illinois bar, John followed his sister Martha, 16 years his senior, west at the age of 24 in 1890. She was a bride of less than a year, having married Superior Court Judge Julius A. Stratton. Powell came by train and joined his brother-in-law's firm, Stratton, Lewis and Gilman.

Powell left in Illinois his betrothed, Elizabeth Gastman, daughter of Enoch A. Gastman, Superintendent of Public Instruction in Decatur. They met in high school and graduated in the same class

The first football game played in Husky Stadium was on November 7, 1930. Courtesy of *Seattle Post Intelligencer.*

from the University of Michigan. A year and a half after coming to
Seattle, Powell felt he had established himself and sent for Elizabeth
to join him. Because there was still no direct rail service to Seattle,
Powell arranged to travel to Spokane to meet Elizabeth when she
arrived from Illinois. They were married in Spokane in February
1892, before making their home in Seattle.

In 1897, Powell was elected from the Third Ward to the Washington State Legislature. He served two terms during the Populist era, as
one of two Republican members. At age 34 in 1900, he and a southern
gentleman named William A. Peters formed the law partnership of
Peters and Powell. This was also the year John and Elizabeth Powell
found a permanent homesite in Madison Park. For the 8 years since
their marriage, they had rented houses, two just south of Madison on
17th and 18th Avenues and another in the Madrona district.

Traveling out on the cable car to the western boundary of Madison Park at 37th Avenue North, and climbing through the woods to
the south, they found their new homestead, covered in virgin timber,
brush, and fallen logs. It seemed to be in the middle of nowhere with
no street on any of the four sides. The Powell family at that time
included 5-year-old Sargent and baby Janet Elizabeth. There were
some doubts as to whether the Powells would really like to live
there—away from their friends, inaccessible, and without even a telephone, but they decided to test it by sort of camping on the property
for the summer. In 10 days' time, they had drawn up a two-story plan,
hired a contractor, built "The Shack," and moved in. The house had
running water, including a bathtub in the kitchen. This was home to
the Powells for 2 years while they planned and built a permanent
house close by.

The Powells' daughter Janet wrote, "We had two big vegetable gardens, so the gardener was employed full-time, although he lived at
home. Jake Bauer lived very near with his family. His wife, Marie, baked
our bread and sometimes came to baby-sit.[21] The Bauers' youngest
child was Janet's age. Eddie Bauer was born on October 19, 1899.

Governor Henry McBride asked John Powell to serve on the University of Washington Board of Regents, where he was instrumental in drawing up the University of Washington Metropolitan Tract Lease. "This obviously important piece of university property between Third and Fifth Avenues, bordered by Seneca to the south and Union on the north—clearly was not being utilized." [22] This land was to become the "new center of Seattle," away from Pioneer Square, an "elite downtown section." Over the next 20 years, its development included the Metropolitan Theater, the Olympic Hotel and Garage, and the White, Henry, Stuart, Cobb, Douglas, Stimson, and Skinner buildings.

John Havard Powell. Sketch by Tom Renton, from a photograph.

Powell was soon named as Chairman of the Committee to confer with the directors of the Alaska–Yukon-Pacific Exposition in regard to the selection of the University grounds as a site for the Exposition to be held in 1909. This required that the campus be leased to the Exposition for the duration of the Fair and that a comprehensive plan be developed for building permanent and temporary structures. Perhaps Washington Park could be laid out as a boulevard entry to the University and the Exposition.

To support this plan, and with enormous foresight and flush with Gold Rush money, Seattle voters approved a $500,000 bond issue for a Park–Boulevard system. This allowed the Parks Commission the next year to hire the eminent John Charles Olmsted of Brookline, Massachusetts, to design a 25-mile citywide park, playground, and boulevard system, preserving and enhancing the beautiful natural landscapes. This legacy ranges from the University campus, to private gardens, to 37 parks, fulfilling Olmsted's ideal of a park or a playground within half a mile of every home.

John Powell's son Sargent attended Dartmouth College and earned his Bachelor and Master's degrees from the University of Washington in 1916, then traveled to the University of Illinois for a doctorate in 1919. He began his teaching career at the University in the Department of Chemistry and taught organic chemistry to generations of University of Washington undergraduates until his retirement in 1963.

MEDICINE AND THE COES

Frantz Hunt Coe and his wife Carrie Everett Coe purchased and lived on the property immediately south of the Powells. Like Powell, Dr. Coe graduated from the University of Michigan, and he came to Seattle shortly after his marriage in 1888. Born in St. Charles, Illinois, in 1856, he was an educator in Michigan before studying medicine. He and his wife had three children. Coe died of kidney failure in 1904, when he was only 48 years old. Coe served as President of the Washington State Medical Society, as well as two terms on the Seattle School Board.

The older of Frantz's two sons, Dr. Herbert Everett Coe, became an associate surgeon of Children's Orthopedic Hospital in 1908. Emilie Bloch Schwabacher wrote, "Dr. Coe was one of the first doctors in the West to be trained as a pediatric surgeon." He "developed new techniques in cleft lip and palate surgical repair...and involved other disciplines in the corrective process such as dentistry and speech therapy."[23]

George Powell remembers that "it was wonderful having Herbert Coe living next to us because he was a highly competent doctor specializing in children's ailments. Whenever anything happened to any of us, he would be glad to come over and take care of it."[24]

On 37th Avenue North, Elizabeth Powell knew the arrival of their third child was imminent and advised her husband, John, that today they would be moving from The Shack into their almost-finished house next door. Achsa Louise (Ah Lou) was born on October 17, 1902, and Dr. Frantz Coe found both mother and baby doing well when he arrived from his home next door.

EARLY SCHOOLS

As the University assumed its responsibilities for higher education, Seattle opened its first high school in 1902. Located at Broadway and Pine Street on a lot purchased by the School Board for $13,000, Seattle High filled a pressing need for the booming city. According to Jacqueline Williams, the massive stone building, designed at a cost of $250,000, welcomed 872 students.[25]

McGilvra School eighth grade class poses on the back steps in 1922, with Archie Anderson on the top step and George Powell in a dark sweater to the right.

Growth in communities along the shores of Lake Washington and their need for schools reflected the city's boom. In the post-fire decade alone, Seattle's population nearly doubled, to 80,671.

A wooden, two-room school house was built in 1899 on property purchased from John McGilvra 8 years earlier. Called The Lake School, the building cost $2,275 and the doors opened to more than 50 students. Homer Turner was the first head teacher. Olive McDougall described the schoolhouse in some detail:[26] There were two classrooms separated by a wide hall. Grades one, two, and three were in one room, and grades four and five were together across the hall. Each classroom had two doors, one at the front and one at the back. The girls' cloakroom was at the front of the school, and the boys' at the back. There were hooks for coats and a shelf for sack lunches. In the girls' cloakroom was a single wash basin with an enamel cup hanging on a chain for drinking water, which served both girls and boys.

The primitive lavatories were in a separate wooden building, shown in an original plan, which is framed and survives today. The building was reached by two paths over two bridges crossing a stream to two ends of the rectangular structure. One door was clearly marked BOYS and the other, GIRLS. The playground had a dirt surface, with woods beyond that.

McDougall recalled that when she started classes at The Lake School, Miss Eva Danzingburg was the teacher for classes one, two, and three. Miss Bertha Heustis taught the fourth- and fifth-grade students across the hall. Miss Danzingburg had additional responsibilities as the Principal.

In Olympia, the state legislature enacted a law in 1903 making school attendance compulsory for children between the ages of 8 and 15.

END OF THE EARLY DAYS

Just before the new millennium, Mount Rainier National Park was established, and Seattle bought Guy Phinney's Woodland Park estate with its wild animal park. The twentieth century in Seattle began with the first automobile on its streets. Ralph Hopkins bought a three-horsepower Woods Electric in Chicago and drove it west.

The Madison Street Cable Car Company continued to serve residents around Lake Washington. From Laurelhurst, businessmen could take an 8-minute ride on the steamer *Sunny Jim* to Madison Park and ride the cable car downtown. (Later, in 1910, Laurelhurst was annexed and came within city limits.) In summer, the cable cars ran every few minutes to Madison Park. In winter, the cars were fitted with removable glass panels that protected passengers from wind and rain. The cable car made these areas "attractive to members of the city's existing elite, to fresh recruits from the East, and to senior white-collar workers who sought to escape the dense, city core."[27]

"Most native-born white men migrated to Seattle from different parts of the state. Illinois and four other Midwestern states contributed the greatest number from outside Washington. The majority of Seattle's foreign-born residents migrated originally from English-speaking countries, or from northern or western Europe, facilitating their assimilation into city life."[28]

Immigrants to Seattle after the turn of the twentieth century, wrote Barbara Hiscock Stenson, were more likely to be young, married women, accompanying their husbands. Those women also were much more likely than Seattle females of previous generations to have been educated beyond grammar or high school. Some had even attended one of the new co-educational public universities in the Midwest. Expansion of intellectual interests among middle and upper class women who had leisure time was reflected in the creation of many women's clubs, whose members were dedicated to cultural self-improvement, education, and civic betterment activities.[29]

Carl F. Wallin and John W. Nordstrom opened their first shoe store at Fourth Avenue and Pike Street in downtown Seattle in 1901.

A hydroelectric dam and plant at Cedar Falls brought the first electric current to Seattle in 1905. Until that time, coal oil lamps were used for light, and wood or coal for heat.

One might say that 1903 marked the end of Seattle's early days and the beginning of its future. It was in this year that John J. McGilvra, founder of much of Madison Park, died at his home at age 76.

Also in 1903, a 22-year-old man from a Detroit lumber and mining family came west to Grays Harbor. His name was William E. Boeing.

On December 17, 1903, Wilbur and Orville Wright's Flyer lifted off in Kitty Hawk, North Carolina. The Wright brothers owned and ran a bicycle shop and had been experimenting for 4 years before finally building a 12-horsepower, four-cylinder motor turning two bicycle chains. The chains, in turn, were linked to two wooden propellers. The pilot lay prone on the lower wing. Orville piloted the first of four flights that historic day and flew the $1000 Wright Flyer 120 feet.

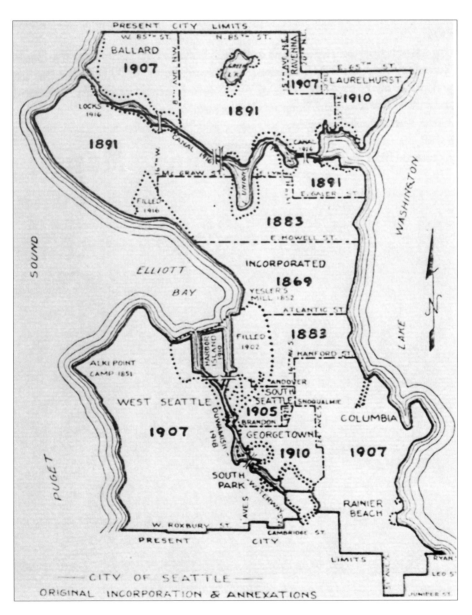

A map of Seattle, from a 1938 WPA project, shows the city's original incorporation and annexations. Courtesy of University of Washington Libraries, Historical Photography Collection. UW 4105

CHAPTER 2

A NEW CENTURY

IN 1907, SEATTLE'S CITY LIMITS stretched from 85th Street to the
north to Roxbury Street in West Seattle and Madison Park continued
to undergo a transformation. Over the years, an area from the
entrance to Washington Park west to 29th Avenue North served as a

The Madison Street trestle looms here as it appeared from Washington Park in 1912. Courtesy of Lawton Gowey and Seattle Municipal Archives.

city dump. In 1905, a trestle, or bridge, was constructed, spanning the ravine. For the next decade the high and wide wooden trestle linked Madison Park to downtown. When the area beneath and around the trestle timbers eventually became filled with all manner of things (mostly garbage), the surface planking was removed from Madison Street and the road was readied to be packed and paved. In this way, Washington Park was reshaped, and in 1909 an amateur baseball field was established there.

POWELL FAMILY RECOLLECTIONS

By 1910, Seattle's population had jumped to 237,194, nearly tripling since 1900. With George's birth, John and Elizabeth Powell's children numbered five. John, Jr. had arrived in 1907.

Older sister Janet wrote, "Our mother was unique among her friends on several points aside from the fact that she lived so far out: She was the only college graduate, had almost the most children and insisted that all of us make the most of every odd hour for education. She taught each of us Latin before we went to High School and we had French, horseback and swimming lessons. The girls had sewing lessons at home and even studied piano for two years to learn the mechanics, make up, of music but the teacher could not understand that Mother did not want us to stay indoors practicing. It should be said that no family could have had more plain fun—strenuous outdoor playing, birthday parties and the wit and humor which emanated constantly from both our parents."[1]

Janet wrote of the importance of horses to living in Madison Park: "Groceries and the Thursday fish-man with his white horse seem to have made it through the woods and up the hill, but it was a long time before we had ice delivery. Through my entire childhood, Sargent [her brother] and I pulled our red wagon down to the Madison cable at 36th where the Conductor heaved our ice out on the ground for us."

The Powells, too, had a white, dual-purpose horse, Queenie. Janet wrote, "My parents harnessed her to the buggy and trotted along the Boulevard a few Sundays and we were supposed to ride her during the week. We built a good sturdy barn with box stalls below and a big carriage room above. It would have held at least three buggies, but the parents soon tired of the Sunday drives and we were certainly not at our best in the saddle. So after a time the equine program was abandoned, Queenie was sold and for a while the barn was empty.

"Our father always said that dogs and gardens didn't go together, so the garden won out. However, we were never without a cat. We tried chickens but they flew at us when we went to feed them. Then we had the rabbit fever, but they were always pushing through the wire netting during the night and making their way, by miraculous instinct, to the lettuce patch."

George Powell, 11 years younger than Janet, wrote in his family history that from 37th Avenue North, "the nearest center of commerce was around 28th and Madison, which was referred to as being 'across the bridge.' There was a drugstore, Weed's hardware store, and a grocery store. My father used to like to smoke cigars and I can remember that often on Sundays he would give me some money and a note to the proprietor of the drugstore and ask me to go across the bridge to buy him some cigars, which I would do, going on foot" as a seven-year-old. [2]

He remembers that, "my father was an avid gardener and we had very extensive gardens. There was a vegetable garden on the north side and on the south side there was an even larger garden. Here there were several large cold frames as well as blackberry vines, raspberry vines, gooseberry plants and currant plants. He raised large amounts of potatoes, peas, corn, beans and smaller amounts of other things such as lettuce, spinach, asparagus, etc. South of the house where "The Shack" used to stand there was a flower garden and then another flower garden on a sort of ledge on the way down to the south garden. At various places in the yard there were fruit trees and I particularly remember the various varieties of cherries around, both pie cherries and sweet cherries. We had a full time gardener, who came six days a week. I can remember his often picking a laundry basket full of fresh peas which then I would shell for the evening meal."

George Powell went on to say, "In those days there was a lot of delivery of necessities to families. First were horse-drawn vehicles and then later, trucks. The principal grocery store in town was Augustine & Kyer. They would telephone our home every weekday morning to get our order. I can clearly remem-

Pandy Christie is pictured beside his truck in Madison Park with fresh fruits and vegetables for sale.

ber my mother talking to them on phone and telling them what she wanted and in due course it would be delivered. Milk, butter, etc. was delivered by another concern, ice in large blocks by yet another concern and fresh fruit and vegetables by a 'vegetable man.' The vegetable man I remember best was Pandy Christie, who continued in business for many years after all other deliveries had stopped." Pandy Christie and his wife Dina came to the United States from Albania in 1917. He made friends with old and young alike while delivering fresh fruits and vegetables in Madison Park until retiring in October, 1972.

In his family history, George Powell wrote about early memories of the land owned by the Puget Mill Company on the north side of Madison Street (later becoming Broadmoor). He remembers that it was referred to as "across Madison."

"It was an unoccupied area with no structures on it and a few skimpy roads and trails. Most of it was wooded but there was an area near the corner of 37th and Madison which was meadowland and every year a few gypsy families would come in the spring and stay there in their covered wagons for quite a few months. So far as I know, they never had permission from anybody, nor did anyone bother them.

Powell recalled that "across Madison" was a playground. "We built small camps over there and tried without much success to trap quail and mountain beaver. We would try to hunt any animal or bird that moved, with homemade slingshots and bows and arrows, without much success. At Christmas time, it was the custom of all the families around the area to go "across Madison" to get their Christmas trees."

On August 20, 1921, John Lehmann led a Mountaineers party of thirteen from Seattle, Tacoma, and Portland, to climb Mount Rainier. Two of those who reached the summit were Sargent Powell and his younger brother John, who had just turned 14.

In the summer of 1922, when George Powell was 12 years old, he swam across Lake Washington from the Tennis Club to Medina. He wrote, "Bob Barr started out with me and Jack Price, whose family

Seattle Tennis Club beach and raft are shown with the *Virginia V* in the background, ca. 1928. Courtesy of Seattle Tennis Club.

owned a home in Medina, rowed a boat along with us in case we tired. Bob Barr did tire and climbed into the boat and they accompanied me for the rest of the trip all the way to Medina and then brought me back. The reason I swam across at that time was that my brother John, who was three years older than I, had accomplished the same feat when he was 12 years old and I felt I had to match what he had done."

While his older siblings went on to Broadway High School, George attended Garfield High School. He wrote, "For my first year there, the buildings were all wooden portables, but the new building was finished in time for the beginning of my second year."

In October 1922, Janet Powell, who graduated from the University of Washington cum laude in 1919, and Neal Tourtellotte, a graduate of the Massachusetts Institute of Technology, were married in Trinity Episcopal Church. At Children's Hospital in 1930, the first official Santa Claus began visiting children who were too ill to go home for the holiday. The one and only Hospital Santa, who came each Christmas morning for the next 30 years, made rounds and distributed gifts. Santa

Santa Claus is photographed on 37th Avenue North following his visit to Children's Orthopedic Hospital on Christmas morning.

wore a red velvet costume trimmed with real ermine that was sewn by his wife—Janet Powell, Mrs. Neal Tourtellotte.

A second sister of John Powell's came to Seattle in 1907. Ellen Powell Dabney, 5 years John's senior, had been a widow for 12 years. While earning a Bachelor of Science degree from the University of Chicago and undertaking postgraduate work at Columbia University, she taught science at Carthage College. Later she taught home economics at Bethel College. Ellen decided to come West with her three youngest children, and she taught home economics at Lincoln High School.

School authorities quickly recognized her ability and in 1911 appointed her director of home economics for the Seattle Public Schools. She held this position for 25 years, until her death in 1937. The *Washington Educational Journal* noted, "With the passing of Ellen Powell Dabney, Seattle loses one of the outstanding pioneers in the home economics movement of forty years ago. She was a fine educator, a noble woman and a nationally known figure."[3]

In March 1930, John Powell was stricken in a King County Superior court room during a trial and died at home a few days later. He was 63. Asked what he considered the most notable characteristics of John Powell, Judge George Donworth responded, "His outstanding legal ability and his staunch integrity of character." Henry Clay Agnew said, "Seattle, and particularly the bar, has lost an illustrious figure. He was never prejudiced by courtroom personalities. He was a formidable opponent in court and a good friend outside." *The Seattle Times* recorded the passing of Powell: "For all his notable attainments and high standing, he remained at heart simple and unspoiled; a kindly and a lovable man. Seattle will miss him sadly and long."[4]

HARNESS RACING

Donald Sherwood wrote that, by 1906, "…the stretch of Arboretum road was the center of the boulevard system and was so popular for autos, carriages, horsemen and pedestrians that a mounted patrolman was necessary. The Park Department furnished the horse and the Police Department the officer."[5] He further reported that a Speedway Organization "raised $9,520 toward the development of a public course (Azalea Way) for the speeding of harness horses together with sheds for cooling the horses and a barn."

Continuing, Sherwood wrote that in 1908, just north of the new Washington Park field, "a stable for eight horses was built, and accommodations for steam rollers and other tools and a headquarters; known as the barn." He noted that horsepower was still the backbone of the Park Department workforce and went on to explain that the "barn became a co-venture as a park service area for tools and horses plus a concession for bridal trails through the Park." The "cooling sheds" were placed near the finish line of the Speedway.

By 1913, the demand for harness racing along the Speedway in the Arboretum had declined. The "horseless carriage" was becoming more and more popular for transportation and for touring. The Riding Academy concession contract expired. Twenty years after its establishment, the Washington Park playfield was expanded with additional fill. Sherwood recorded that the original plans of the Arboretum Agreement called for a rose garden at this site, but in 1929 the community protested giving up any of the playfield for roses. Most significant, fill operations were moved north of the Ship Canal to the west side of Union Bay

CHILDREN'S ORTHOPEDIC HOSPITAL
AND ANNA HERR CLISE

In Seattle a mother, Anna Herr Clise, was searching for a way to help sick and crippled children, having lost her 5-year-old son to inflammatory rheumatism. Clise, originally from Lancaster, Pennsylvania, consulted with her cousin, Dr. John Musser of Philadelphia, President of the American Medical Association, who told her, "There's nothing so important to be done as service to children. Look about and see what is being done for them in your state. Find out what is not being done that is necessary and worthy, and do that."[6] According to Emilie Schwabacher, for 25 years a Trustee of Children's Orthopedic Hospital, Clise invited 23 women to become partners with her in the endeavor. Everyone present opened her purse, put up ten dollars and pledged a second ten dollars within the year."

Children's Orthopedic Hospital Association Ward in Seattle opened the first orthopedic facility for children on the West Coast in February 1907. It was relocated on Queen Anne Hill in 1911. Later, Elizabeth Powell became a member of the Children's Orthopedic

Hospital Board, serving from 1920 to 1944. This active and dedicated group of women met regularly and often in response to the increasing needs of children. George Powell remembers that, when he was old enough to drive, he took his mother from Madison Park across town to Queen Anne Hill for Hospital Board meetings.

James William Clise, husband of Anna, was a businessman and horse breeder who became chairman of the original Western Washington Fair and Round-up. These riding and roping events took place on the baseball field/fairgrounds just north of Madison Street. Bruce Shorts remembers that even a small circus used the grounds, giving young boys the opportunity to sneak in under the tents. He chuckles today at thoughts of the sideshow poster featuring a boy, "Schlitzie, The Brainless Wonder"—a name that Shorts quickly applied to his younger brother Calhoun.[7]

THE 1909 EXPOSITION

The Milwaukee Railroad over Snoqualmie Pass, completed in 1909, provided one more link with the rest of the country just in time to celebrate the June 1 opening of the Alaska–Yukon-Pacific Exposition, attended by 79,000 people. The Fair was planned to display the resources, products, and advantages of Washington and the region. The Exposition lasted 6 months and celebrated the 12 years of prosperity following the 1897 Alaska Gold Rush.

During the Exposition, the park at the foot of Madison Street was renamed "White City Park." Olive McDougall remembers attending as a seven-year-old and seeing every building outlined in lights.[8] The site included, of course, the necessary merry-go-round, Ferris wheel, roller coaster, and penny arcade. A miniature train was available for rides.

President William Howard Taft arrived to close the Exposition and spoke to at least 25,000 spectators on the university campus. By the time of the Exposition's closing, 3.7 million people had visited over a 138-day span.

BROADMOOR—VERNON MACAN AND
CHARLES HANLY BADGLEY

Thirty years have passed, Forrest Richardson wrote, since the Puget Mill Company logged its Washington Park property.[9] Golf had been gaining in popularity for about a decade, so an 18-hole course with homesites seemed to be an ideal use for 216 acres of the property. In 1926, the Puget Mill Company sold, to Broadmoor Golf Club Corporation, 400 residential lots around the new U-shaped golf course designed by A. Vernon Macan.

According to Jeff Mingay's article, Macan was born in Dublin in 1882, studied law at Trinity College, and was married in 1911. His passion for golf interfered with his attention to the practice of law.[10] Macan left for Victoria in 1912 and promptly won the British Columbia amateur title. Macan volunteered for World War I service in 1916, was trained as a machine-gunner, and fought in the April 1917 assault on Vimy Ridge in France. He was hit and sustained a serious foot injury that resulted in his left leg being amputated below the knee.

During a long recuperation in Dublin, Macan studied golf course design and construction. Following the Armistice, Macan returned to British Columbia and the next day won a golf tournament. His handicap had risen by only two strokes. Macan believed that wide fairways and large, rolling greens appealed to golfers of all abilities. Between 1922 and 1925, he was the busiest golf course designer in the Pacific Northwest.

While a student at the University, Charles Hanly Badgley worked one summer shoulder to shoulder with other young men, raking dirt the length of Broadmoor and back, preparing the fairways for seeding and landscaping. The middle of three sons, Badgley had moved from West Virginia to Seattle with his family when he was very young. His father had trained at Johns Hopkins as a doctor, but medicine was not a profitable profession at that time. The Badgleys were drawn to the West with the promise of real estate opportunities in Seattle. Following his marriage, Charles built a home in Madison Park, where he and his family lived for 10 years.

The Puget Mill Company agreed to contribute substantially to the construction of a clubhouse. The development was promoted as a "Country Club within the City." In a 1927 newspaper account, Almira Bailey wrote of "Broadmoor, acres of exclusiveness, that was a few months ago covered with lowly sallal and fireweed."[11] She continued, "In the early days East Madison was just a little moist, woodsy road through miles of forest to the lake. And now broad boulevards lead to stately homes."

BROADMOOR'S EARLY ARCHITECTURE

Architect John Graham, Sr. was hired in 1927 to design the clubhouse at Broadmoor. According to author Grant Hildebrand, Graham was born in Liverpool in 1873 and came to Seattle in 1901.[12] Like many architects of his generation, he gained his experience through apprenticing rather than through formal education. Graham became the most prolific commercial architect in Seattle.

The first private home in this residential park was built by C. Edwin Davis.[13] Davis was born in Hugaton, Kansas, in 1888. He graduated from the University of Oklahoma in 1896 and worked for the government on both the East Coast and the West Coast. He married Augusta Caldwell Bright, from Louisville, Kentucky, in 1917, and they moved to Seattle in 1920, where Davis began work as a public accountant for Price Waterhouse. The couple had two daughters, then a son.

A story about their Broadmoor house—which may or may not be true—is that Augusta was less than enthusiastic about moving to Seattle. Her husband purportedly promised her he would build her a home just like the Georgian Colonial house they were leaving in Virginia's Shenandoah Valley. To further appease his wife, Edwin asked the Broadmoor Corporation to rename the street where their new home stood. It is today Shenandoah Drive. The Davises lived there until 1937, when they moved to California.

The architectural firm of Schack, Young and Myers was retained in 1926 to design the Davis house. James H. Schack was born in the Schleswig region of Germany in 1871 and came to Seattle in 1901. Arrigo M. Young was born in London in 1884, received a bachelor of science degree from the University of Michigan, and came to Seattle in 1910. David J. Myers was born in Glasgow, Scotland, in 1872, came to Seattle with his family in 1889, and later studied architecture at the Massachusetts Institute of Technology. According to David Rash, the firm "had a well-established reputation for commercial buildings" by the mid-1920s.[14]

At that time, the city was booming. In 1920, Seattle, with a population of 327,194, ranked as the third largest city west of the Mississippi, behind only San Francisco and Los Angeles.

CIVIC ADVANCES AND MARK REED

Washington State granted woman suffrage in 1910. For the first time, women had the right to vote in the city elections of 1911. Politicians and special interest groups had to face 20,000 or more new voters who were unwilling to tolerate unsavory and illicit businesses.

Historian Richard Berner explained that "Seattle (and Washington as a whole) had drawn together a fresh middle class that had not yet developed a stake in sustaining the inequalities and inequities that existed in the older cities of the nation's East and Midwest. As it advanced its own welfare and moral values, this middle class leaned toward a more humane vision of society that gave support to a whole range of civic improvements. That members of this social stratum were active voters must not be overlooked."[15]

The year 1911 marked the passage of Washington's Workmen's Compensation Act, which, Berner wrote, "would become the national standard it was so well written."[16] Along with other lumbermen and mine owners, Mark Reed from Shelton had lobbied the legislature for passage of this bill. Still, the Workman's Compensation

Act compensated an injured worker only for lost wages; it made no provision for medical expenses.

Upon the death of Alfred Anderson, Mark Reed assumed the presidency of the Simpson Logging Company in 1914. At age 58, Reed was suddenly "one of the region's major financial figures," wrote historian Robert Ficken, with ownership responsibilities extending to railroads, banking, and transportation.[17] Beginning a 16-year career as a Washington state legislator, Reed was elected to represent Mason County in 1915. He is quoted as saying, "Personally, I think every good citizen has a duty to uphold in the community. Some of us, due to a more fortunate position, have a larger duty than others, but we all can, and should, help."

Reed sponsored the state's first medical insurance act, establishing a state medical board to administer employer–employee contributions and pay the doctors' bills for injured workers. Midway through his term in Olympia, in 1923, he served as Speaker of the House. Through fluctuations in the lumber markets, Reed continued to demonstrate commitment to Shelton and to loggers and their families, by providing the comforts of the camps, the construction of schools, and the establishment of health insurance for his employees.

A graduate of the California Military Academy in 1887, Reed had a profound respect for the value of discipline and an ordered existence. He said later that military training "tends to impress upon the youth the necessity of obeying their superiors and brings to their attention their obligation to promptly act when a definite purpose is set before them for consummation."[18]

Reed sent all three of his sons from Shelton to Indiana to attend the Culver Military Academy. According to Robert Spector, Mark Reed's dream was for his logging interests to be run by his two older sons, Sol and Frank. Bill was the youngest and the third to graduate, in 1925.[19]

THE SHIP CANAL AND MONTLAKE BRIDGE

For decades, ideas and plans had been put forth pertaining to a canal that would join Lake Washington and Shilshole Bay. Logs and coal were both being moved from the Lake to Elliott Bay in a laborious manner. The logs were sluiced through a narrow, muddy ditch to Lake Union, lying 9 feet lower than Lake Washington. Coal had to be barged and then portaged over land to Elliott Bay. General Hiram M. Chittenden of the United States Army Corps of Engineers recommended "a system with two locks, one larger than the other, with the smaller one intended to accommodate Seattle's 'mosquito fleet' and small craft".[20] In 1911, the Lake Washington Ship Canal construction began at its saltwater terminus.

The Montlake Cut was completed in August 1916 with its connection to Lake Union's Portage Bay. For two months, fresh water from Lake Washington was released slowly through the manmade Cut to the lower Lake Union. Lake Washington's shoreline, dramat-

Lake Union's Portage Bay is flooding into the Montlake Cut in 1916. Courtesy of Paul Dorpat.

ically altered, was for the most part 9 vertical feet lower. The south outfall of Lake Washington, which ran to the Duwamish River by way of the Black River, was eliminated. In many areas, great expanses of lake bottom were exposed and many square feet of desirable new lakefront real estate were now available. Madison Park Beach was created by the shore east of what had been Laurel Shade Avenue. In the following year, the Lake Washington Ship Canal was completed to the Government Locks, and the vision of the pioneer fathers, a waterway between Puget Sound and Lake Washington, was realized.

The Montlake bridge was built in 1925. This enabled Madison Park residents to travel north in the city without having to go downtown as far as 8th Avenue, north along Eastlake, and across the University bridge.

THE ARBORETUM

In 1929, the Great Depression rendered the University of Washington unable to proceed with plans for the Arboretum. [21] Members of the Seattle Garden Club raised $3,000 as a commission for James Frederick Dawson, lead designer for the Olmsted Brothers of Massachusetts, to prepare a master plan.

PUBLIC SCHOOLS—FRANK B. COOPER AND EDGAR BLAIR

Frank B. Cooper was 11 years into his 21-year term as the city's Superintendent of Public Instruction, historian Berner reported, when he saw "an opportunity to build the system as the city itself grew. This was in contrast with his counterparts elsewhere who had to contend with established populations, political machines and social institutions."[22]

The new Lake School was one of 44 new schools built since 1902, most of which were constructed of brick. The principal architect for these educational facilities was Edgar Blair, who had come to Seattle from Iowa and adapted a basic nine-room plan to many of the school sites. The new elementary school for Madison Park was opened to students in 1913 and cost $75,627. By the following year, the playground was graded at an additional cost of $3,100.

The brick schoolhouse in Madison Park was renamed the J. J. McGilvra School in honor of the pioneer who had contributed in so many ways to the neighborhood, the city, and the state. In 1914, the school had 155 students enrolled in grades one through seven B. The seven A (second semester of seventh grade) and eighth grades were introduced to McGilvra in 1918.

In 1940, 28 years after the school was constructed, four additional classrooms were extended from the north side of the old brick building, at a cost of $26,429. Madison Park needed more classrooms, and the neighborhood's growth justified adding the "new wing."

The youngest of John and Elizabeth Powell's children graduated from McGilvra School in 1922. Reflecting on his years at McGilvra, George Powell remembers that "there were a number of students from the east side of the Lake, i.e., Hunts Point, Yarrow Point, Evergreen Point, Medina, etc. The children were brought to McGilvra School by a small steamer called the *Ariel* which would deposit them at the foot of Madison Street (a few blocks from the school) early in the morning and pick them up when school was over in the afternoon and take them home."[23]

George Powell recalls that his second-grade teacher was Miss Marie Nettleton and that Miss Danzingburg was the principal. "Once in a while when my parents went away on a trip they would have one of the teachers come and stay in the house with us children…. The persons with whom I played when not in school—all through grade school and high school—were the boys that lived near me on what was generally referred to as 'the hill.' There were lots of boys my age—enough to form a football team or a baseball team, but oddly enough, only a few girls of that age."

THE MUSIC PALACE

Madison Park lost an important landmark in March of 1914: The Music Palace of Washington, which had welcomed audiences for 24 years, burned. During what would be its final year, the stage was illuminated with new electric lights. Olive McDougall recalls seeing the wooden pavilion in flames from a classroom window at the school. She also remembers the sound of the big gray fire horses and the fire wagon racing to this and many other fires that were common in early Madison Park, with its dependence on coal oil lamps.[24]

AVIATION—EDDIE HUBBARD AND WILLIAM BOEING

In 1913, a pusher flying boat, built from Curtiss plans, was moved from Everett to Madison Park immediately south of Washington Pioneer Hall. Jim Brown wrote that Terah T. Maroney and Leo "Dutch" Huber collaborated successfully with Eddie Hubbard to design the ship's capability as a land-plane.[25] It was the forerunner of the amphibian idea. At age 24, Hubbard was trained as an engineer and a pilot, and in 1915 he became the first graduate of the Aviation School in the Northwest. He flew the float plane out of the hangar at Madison Park. Powered by a Curtiss 60-horsepower engine, the plane reached 55 mph when aloft.

In 1916, William Boeing built his first plane, a twin-float bi-plane, beside Lake Union in his boathouse. Boeing had moved from Grays Harbor to Seattle in 1908 and, in 1910, bought a shipyard on the Duwamish River, known today as the "Red Barn." A year before building his bi-plane, Boeing had his first plane ride, with Maroney at the controls. In July of the same year, Pacific Aero Products Company was incorporated and Boeing bought most of the stock issued. Operations were moved to the Duwamish site, and in less than a year, the company name was changed to the Boeing Airplane Company.

A recent engineering graduate from the University of Washington, Philip G. Johnson joined the Boeing Company in June of 1917. The next month, the U. S. Navy, now at war, placed an order with

Boeing for 50 seaplane trainers. At this time, 337 employees were on the Boeing Company payroll.

In 1919, the 30-year-old lead test pilot, Eddie Hubbard, who had worked for the Boeing Company for 3 years, initially as a mechanic, flew the first international airmail flight from Vancouver, British Columbia, to the company's hangar on Lake Union. Flying with Hubbard in his own private C-700 seaplane was William Boeing. The flight was a part of the Canadian Exposition, and the men were carrying a bag holding 60 pieces of mail. The trip took 3 hours each way and included stops.

William Boeing and Eddie Hubbard stand with the mailbag following their historic international flight in 1919. Courtesy of Museum of History and Industry, Seattle. SHS 12544

Hubbard left Boeing Company a year and a half later and bought the company's first Boeing-designed commercial aircraft. With financial backing from two Boeing executives, Vice President Edgar Gott and General Manager Phil Johnson, Hubbard bought the one and only B-1 flying boat from Boeing. The two Boeing executives became his partners in this new enterprise, Hubbard Air Transport Company.

Hubbard, under contract for routine airmail service, logged 220 accident-free trips between Seattle and Victoria before returning to Boeing in 1923 as a test pilot. Both Gott and Johnson went on to become presidents of Boeing.

Between 1919 and 1924, the Boeing Company built 298 de Havillands. Eddie Hubbard, who died in 1928 at age 39, is remembered as the man who put Boeing in the commercial field of aviation.

The decade of the 1920s has been referred to as "the years of airplanes and automobiles." Early in 1927, the Boeing Airplane Company won the contract to fly airmail between Chicago and San Francisco for the U. S. Postal Department. The next year the National Broadcasting Company (NBC) began a coast-to-coast radio network, and Boeing proudly advertised that its passengers would now travel in comfort with stewardesses/nurses in attendance on the flights. Coast-to-coast mail and passenger services were introduced in 1931, when Boeing Air Transport combined with three other airlines to become United Air Lines. The coast-to-coast trip took 27 hours one way.

WORLD WAR I

In 1917, President Woodrow Wilson asked Congress for a Declaration of War against Germany. On April 6, the United States joined Britain, its colonies, dominions, and allies in what became known as the Great War. Two months later, Major General John J. Pershing led American troops into France

In a letter home to his family, 23-year-old Army Captain Neal Everett Tourtellotte, stationed in France with the newly developed Tractor Artillery, wrote, "The service I am in now is a combination of Field or Light Artillery along with Heavy Artillery. We have all the mobility of the horse-drawn battery—their dash, speed and excitement, including danger; coupled with the science of the big guns since our cannons are all large size."[26]

In another letter he wrote, "Often while walking down the street, old gentlemen would stop us, gravely salute, shake us by the hand and then in slowly spoken French or broken English tell us how glad they were to see us over here to help them and how much they appreciated our assistance in the great fight for "Liberté."

By the end of World War I with an Armistice signed, the allied forces had won, but had incurred 5,152,115 deaths. Of this number 116,000, lost in just 18 months, were Americans.

THE SMITH TOWER—LYMAN C. SMITH

Seattle, touted as the "fastest growing city in America," celebrated the opening of the tallest building west of the Mississippi River in 1914. Lyman C. Smith, a businessman from Syracuse, visited Seattle in 1909 and was anxious to invest in this western city and promote sales for his Smith Typewriter Company. Brothers Edwin H. and T. Walter Gaggin, graduates of the School of Architecture of Syracuse University, were hired to design the Smith Tower. The white building at Second Avenue and Yesler rose 42 floors, the first two of which were finished in Washington granite and the higher stories in terra cotta. The Smith Tower dominated Seattle's skyline from 1914 until 1962, when the Space Needle replaced it as the highest structure against the skyline.

A PRESIDENTIAL VISIT AND AN HISTORIC FLIGHT

In July 1923, President Warren Harding spoke to a packed Husky stadium while he was on a stop-over in Seattle during a trip back to Washington, D.C. from Alaska. Deciding to greet the President at his West Coast visit was 32-year-old 2nd Lt. Edward Henry McGehee Morrison, Air Service Reserves, who would complete the first dawn to dusk flight from Los Angeles to Seattle. He wrote in the Log that Army Air Service 1st Lt. C. C. Moseley was at the controls of the single engine DeHavilland bi-plane powered by a 420-horsepower Liberty engine.[27]

Brothers Edward and Jay Morrison are pictured with their sisters in Hollywood in 1918.

Moseley was challenging the Navy's boast that it would send a squadron of nine air-planes from North Island, San Diego, to Seattle to greet the first President to visit the Territory of Alaska. "Three of us finally turned the prop over. In total darkness we had our last bounce off Clover Field in Santa Monica at 4:15 am. Because of my previous training as a newspaper photographer, Moseley desired that I accompany him on the trip. I secured my uniform from the Studio Wardrobe and borrowed a Grayflex from a down-town supply house. Sitting on this parachute, I settled down for a long day."

The first stop was Sacramento, the second was Eugene, and 11 air hours later, Seattle. The highest altitude reached was 10,000 feet when alongside Mt. Shasta. "We start down. I try for a picture of Sand Point Field, which is a swath cut out of the forest."

Continuing his account, Morrison wrote, "It has been a pioneer trip and well within reason to predict that the same trip will become more and more frequent in the very near future. Out of the squadron of nine naval ships, two landed at Sand Point Field at Seattle five days after leaving North Island, San Diego. The remainder of the squadron is somewhere between here and there."

He continued to enter in the Log that "Mr. Gott, of the Boeing Airplane Company of Seattle, greeted us at the Field, and the hospitality of Seattle is truly wonderful. The next morning, July 27, due to the late arrival of the Presidential party, the reception at the pier was cancelled. As the President and Mrs. Harding stepped off the gang plank they were greeted by the Governor and Mrs. Hart, the Mayor and Mrs. Brown, and the President of the Chamber of Commerce. The Mayor says, 'Mose,' and called him over to meet the President and told the President that 'Mose' had made the dawn to dusk flight from Los Angeles, whereupon the President congratulated Moseley upon accomplishing such a flight and said, "Evidently you are as much of a man as you look. May I present Mrs. Harding?'"

After greeting Mrs. Harding, the Presidential party members were taken to their automobile, and they started on their parade through the city. "While Seattle is a fine city, and I desire to go there again, we had done our business and were anxious to start home.

"July 28, 4:08 A.M. We warm up. As the first few minutes of our homeward hop is to be over water (Lake Washington and Puget Sound) 'Mose' tells me not to hook my parachute harness until we have been up for ten or fifteen minutes, because one of the characteristics of the Liberty Motor is that, if it does not cut in the first ten minutes of flying, it will generally carry you through. If we have a forced landing while over water it will be easier to swim out without a parachute around you."

And, after leaving Eugene, "Due to the cool of the morning and the fact that we were going up at least 10,000 feet to get by Mt. Shasta, we both crawl into our fur-lined flying suits. The parachute harness and safety belt holds the flying suit very close to the body. Mather Field, Sacramento, spotted ahead. We shut down and land. 'Mose' and I crawled out of the ship, got out of the flying suits as fast as possible, both of us were wringing wet with perspiration. Temperature 105 in the shade—temperature unknown inside our fur-lined flying suits. 6:20 P.M. We are down. Total flying time on return trip—10 hours.

"We wonder where the seven Navy ships that did not make it to Seattle are.

"The salient features of the trip that impressed me are:

The Pilot.

The need of a Pacific Coast Airway.

The performance of the ship.

Photographic conditions."

One week later, on August 2, the presidential boat reached San Francisco, where Warren Harding died the same day. Five months later, in Los Angeles, 2nd Lt. Edward Morrison died from a routine, but tainted, Army Air Service inoculation. A letter, written on Christmas Day from his grieving sister Mary to another sister Ethel, reads, "It just breaks one's heart to think of the days and weeks of suffering. It seems such a tragedy that one so young as Edward, and especially one who loved life and action as he loved them, should be stilled forever."[28]

Major C.C. Moseley, former World War I fighter pilot, became a co-founder of Western Air Express, later named Western Airlines.

EDDIE BAUER

Among the first students to enroll in the new McGilvra School facility was a boy who was born and spent his early years on Orcas Island. His parents immigrated there from Russia in 1889 and then moved to a house on 37th Avenue North in Madison Park. His name was Eddie Bauer.

Second Avenue was the city's main retail street. The young Eddie Bauer, barely out of his teens, opened his first store, Eddie Bauer's Tennis Shop, in 1920, at Second and Seneca. By 1928, Bauer had introduced Norwegian hickory skis and instructors to Seattle. In an article about Eddie Bauer, Robert Spector wrote that during that winter, Bauer went on a midwinter steelhead fishing trip with a friend. They were dressed in fine woolen jackets, but Bauer sent his

Eddie Bauer is shown with his catch of the day, ca. 1924. © 2004 Eddie Bauer Inc.

heavy jacket on ahead with the friend while he carried the weight of their successful catch. Bauer became drowsy with hypothermia and believed he owed his survival to the fact that he could communicate distress to his friend by firing three shots in the air.[29]

That experience reminded Bauer of an uncle's story of his and other Russian officers crediting the down-insulated lining of their coats with saving their lives in the Russo–Japanese war of 1904. Temperatures plunged to 50 degrees below zero in Manchuria. Bauer "designed and sewed a quilted down jacket for himself and later made similar garments for a few of his hunting friends. The jackets were so popular that he patented the design." He called that first model the Skyliner. Today it continues to be one of the best sellers in the Eddie Bauer catalog.

Like most businesses during the years following Pearl Harbor, Bauer's sales were disrupted by requisition. In his article, Spector quoted Bauer as saying that, from 1942 on, "all the down went to the war-production board. They asked me to get thousands of sleeping bags of any kind and description and some 25,000 flight suits (insulated to keep a motionless person comfortably warm at 70 degrees below zero)."[30] By the end of the war, everyone knew about Eddie Bauer's down outerwear—in most cases by word of mouth. He was able to move quickly into peacetime production for sportsmen.

CHAPTER 3

THE DEPRESSION AND WORLD WAR II

THE DAYS LEADING UP TO WORLD WAR II and the War itself saw many changes in Seattle, and many residents of Madison Park were deployed or contributed to wartime efforts in other ways. Much of this chapter is presented through the words of Madison Park residents who served in the war. First, though, one year in particular was marred by catastrophe.

1933—A MOMENTOUS YEAR

In Shelton, 28-year-old Sol Reed, married just a year, stopped at his brother Frank's front porch on the way home from work. A crippled and embittered Simpson logger fired four shots from across the street, and Reed died shortly after reaching the hospital. His assassin succumbed less than an hour later, of a self-inflicted revolver wound. Robert Spector wrote that Sol's father, Mark Reed, permanently moved the family to Seattle, declaring, "We've had enough. It is just too awful to contemplate."[1] Spector added, "Bill's life changed radically with Sol's death. At his father's request, Bill left Harvard, abandoned his banking career, and returned to Shelton to learn the forest products business."

Later that year Mark Reed returned to Seattle from a meeting in Chicago, where he had met with industry leaders at the Congress

Hotel. What he attributed to "a rough flight and lack of sleep" turned out to be amoebic dysentery contracted from a food handler at the hotel. Mark Edward Reed died in 1933 at age 67.

A celebration in that time of tragedy was the marriage of George Powell, a University of Washington law student, and Katherine Jaynes in August of 1933 at the Church of the Epiphany. The two had met over summer vacation 9 years earlier on the raft at the Tennis Club.

In another loss in 1933, the white frame house on the shores of Lake Washington known as Laurel Shade, owned by Caroline McGilvra Burke,

Mark Edward Reed, ca. 1930. Courtesy of the Reed family.

burned, at a loss of $1,000. It had been rented to the T.D. Foleys.

Reed's widow, Irene Simpson Reed, bought a Lakefront portion of the McGilvra homestead along 42nd Avenue North, from Lee to Garfield Streets. Her son Frank was married to Georgine, and they had two boys. Bill (William G.), married Eleanor Henry in 1935, at age 30. In the spring of 1940, within a 6-week period, death came to the matriarchs of the Simpson Logging Company—Mary Garrard Simpson and her daughter, Irene Simpson Reed.

THE WPA: THE ARBORETUM AND THE LAND USE SURVEY

President Franklin Delano Roosevelt introduced the New Deal in 1933. Among the 8,000 parks across the nation benefiting from the Works Progress Administration (WPA) was the Washington Park Arboretum, for which 800 laborers and other resources were utilized in 1936 for its development. Thomas Veith wrote that Lester P. Fey, at that time a 36-year-old partner of Arthur Lamont Loveless, designed the Arboretum Gatehouse in the style of an English cottage. Cobblestones removed from Madison Street were used to build the cottage and other architectural features within the Park.[2]

The King County Assessor's Office was granted additional WPA funds to conduct a Land Use Survey, and 300–400 people found jobs gathering information on structures and properties throughout the county. The Survey was under way in Madison Park in 1937. The information gathered included photographs of businesses and homes, which provided a valuable record, now stored at the Puget Sound Regional Branch of the Washington State Archives.

The result of the Survey, finished in 1940, was "a dramatic gain of assessed real estate valuation," which greatly added to the county's tax base.[3] The Survey was the largest white-collar WPA project to be carried out in King County

With the help of WPA workers and dollars, the Madison Park Bath House underwent a remodel during this period. Since the Depression, it has served as a multi-service facility for the community.

PUBLIC TRANSPORTATION AND THE FLOATING BRIDGE

Two important developments in public transportation were under way in Seattle in 1940. The cable car system was converted to electric "trackless trolleys" with the power running on overhead wires. Also, the Lake Washington Floating Bridge—named 27 years later for the director of the State Department of Highways, Lacey V. Morrow, a brother of journalist Edward R. Morrow—opened after many skeptics had said, "She'll never float." This highway connection between Seattle and Mercer Island was supported by concrete pontoons. Taylor Scott remembers riding bicycles with Tom Youell from Madison Park to Leschi and along the tunnel's pedestrian walkway at the west end of the bridge.[4]

The particular impact on Madison Park was that, even with a toll on the new bridge, automobile traffic chose to cross Lake Washington

The ferry *Leschi* is departing from Kirkland and heading to Madison Park, 1940s. Courtesy of Bart Ripp and www.historylink.org

by the bridge rather than wait for the ferry. The *Lincoln* was retired in 1940. The smaller *Leschi* was updated and began service from Madison Park to Kirkland, which continued until 1950. The Mercer Island bridge toll had been removed the year before. By this time, nearly 1,200 passengers a day were making the 30-minute ferry commute, at a cost of 10 cents for a pedestrian and 25 cents for a car and driver. Mitzi Balkema Hagan and her son James were on the last round-trip run on August 31, Jim riding comfortably in his stroller.[5]

BEGINNING OF THE WAR

James Burns wrote that in July, 1941, "The United States crossed the threshold from peace to war; as the war widened in Europe, the Atlantic lifeline came under attack, the British sought more aid, public opinion changed to favor more interventions, and defense production pulled the United States out of the depression."[6]

INTERNMENT CAMPS—THE YAMAGUCHIS

Early in 1942, after the United States entered World War II, paranoia and fear drove the American leadership to create ten "relocation centers" out of vast, barren land. Presidential Executive Order 9066 called for the removal of American citizens of Japanese descent from the West Coast. In all, 110,000 people along the Pacific Coast were sent first to "assembly centers" before being moved east by train to internment camps.

Among the 9,397 people of Japanese descent sent to the internment camp in Hunt, Idaho, were Jack and Dorothy Yamaguchi from Seattle. They were married in April, 1942, and 4 months later were on the train to 950 acres of wasteland surrounded by barbed wire, guard towers, armed guards, and watchdogs: This was Minidoka. With but one week's notice to get their affairs in order, the internees were ordered away for no one knew how long. Tar-paper barracks, with no insulation and no running water, awaited Jack and Dorothy. He worked as a business manager in the camp office of the newspaper and saved most of the photographs. These images have made possible the remembering and telling the story of one of America's darkest moments.[7] Three years later the Yamaguchis, then with two toddlers, returned to Seattle. As a side note, a family member of theirs has owned a business in Madison Park for many years.

In January of 1943, Secretary of War Henry L. Stimson announced that men of Japanese ancestry between the ages of 17 and 37 would have the opportunity to serve in a combat unit for active service in the theater of war. More than 300 men from Minidoka volunteered. Their unit, the 442 Regimental Combat Team, fought in the Italian campaign and was the most decorated unit of WWII.

THE WAR YEARS—JOHN POWELL, JR.,
AND BRUCE SHORTS

According to James Warren, a group of Seattle businessmen decided the city needed a center point to raise money and morale for the war effort.[8] Victory Square, on University Street between 4th and 5th Avenues, was dedicated on May 2, 1942. At the west end of the Square, the domed speaker's stand resembled Thomas Jefferson's Monticello, and at the east end, the 75-foot-high obelisk was a replica of the Washington Monument. An enormous crowd turned out for the dedication and, while an Army band played patriotic songs, began buying war bonds.

Throughout the war, visiting Hollywood movie stars and big bands provided entertainment for the crowds and support for the war effort. By the end of the war in 1945, the monument was covered with the inscribed names of those from King County who lost their lives in the war.

Like many young men, John H. Powell, Jr., then 34-years-old, submitted an Application for Commission in the U.S. Naval Reserve in 1942.[9] He was a 1929 graduate of the Massachusetts Institute of Technology with majors in Electrical and Mechanical Engineering and work experience in the design and detailing of marine deck machinery. Lt. Powell was sent to San Diego for training, and then was assigned to the South Pacific as the Commander for Service Division 72, Service Force, Pacific Fleet.

The Navy established a large facility on the Island of Manos in the Admiralty Islands, as it was not practical for ships to have to go to Honolulu or to the mainland for repairs. Adjoining the facility was a plant that produced oxy-acetylene for use in metal-cutting torches, and Powell was in charge of that unit. His Honorable Discharge papers are dated January 30, 1946, and he was as thrilled as anyone in uniform to be going home.

Bruce Shorts was born in Seattle in 1909 and graduated from Stanford University in 1931 and the University of Michigan Law School in 1934. He married Beryl Elfendahl in 1938 and moved to Madison Park with his wife and twin daughters the next year. Shortly after Pearl Harbor, he had the first of many encounters that resulted in a military career that was notable for several significant incidents.[10]

A friend, Charles Pye "Bert" Burnett, Jr., introduced Shorts to the idea of putting his law degree to use as a Judge Advocate in the Army. Shorts received enlistment papers and was deployed to Fort Sam Houston with the 95th Division and the rank of Captain. As he was checking in with the superior officer, a man arrived from the 3rd Army's Operations Section, looking for one more officer to attend Command Staff School. "Take him," the officer said, and a few days later Shorts left for Command Staff School at the University of Michigan. He returned there, this time for 10–12 weeks' training as a Judge Advocate.

After completing this course, he was assigned to the 95th Division as an assistant to the Division Judge Advocate General. The Army was engaged in the takeover of a plant that had gone on strike. Civilian manufacturing companies were learning that the war effort took precedence over unions. When Shorts expressed surprise at such an interesting assignment, Burnett confessed that he was head of the Selection Committee.[10] Burnett, a son-in-law of Seattle pioneer Joshua Green, was attached to the Office of the Secretary of State. While on assignment, Colonel Burnett's plane went down on Florida Island near Guadalcanal in a storm. Burnett died just days before his 40th birthday.[11]

Shorts was sent overseas to Winchester, England, in 1944, where he was responsible for supplying drivers from his Division to help implement the "Red Ball Express." Following D Day, the Allies were moving quickly and there was urgency in keeping the troops supplied with food, fuel, and arms. Trucks ran night and day from the beaches to wherever they were needed in Europe and back to the Coast again. As the allied forces advanced, the supply trucks ran from France into Holland and then to Germany.

While in England, Shorts learned that his younger brother Calhoun, a Naval officer whom he had not seen for more than a year, was on a ship near Weymouth. With difficulty, Shorts arranged a reunion for the two in Winchester just before Cal was rotated back to the

States. During that reunion, Shorts learned that Cal had been in charge of a Landing Craft Infantry (LCI) and on June 6, 1944, was on one of the lead boats into the beach at Normandy. Cal was on his way back to the States because the LCI operation was being turned over to the British Navy. During that brief reunion, Cal gave Shorts his heavy, hooded, alpaca-lined seafaring coat.

As an interesting historic note, Cal Shorts designed, and the Navy adopted, LCI racks that could hold the rafts. These racks permitted rafts to be launched directly into the English Channel rather than their having to be hoisted over a rail. This maneuver could be executed much faster and at less risk to the troops aboard. Cal's skill and ability at knowing tides and currents, learned during his years sailing on Puget Sound, was of enormous value to the Navy on D Day.[12]

Landing on Omaha Beach, then moving to combat in Holland, Bruce Shorts was notified that he was needed at Headquarters, where he was to be a liaison with the British ("You're the only one who has been to Command and General Staff Schools"). His new duties were to coordinate combined operations with the U.S. and the British 43rd. This assignment continued until the allied troops were through the Siegfried Line. The British 43rd had been in North Africa and had developed a code for radio communication. As liaison, Shorts was given information from the British Division, which he passed on to his division.

When he was a Judge Advocate, Shorts came across Navajo soldiers with no written language, who were charged with going AWOL but actually were lost. In trying to move through the train stations, most were handicapped by not being able to read or speak English. Shorts appealed to the General on their behalf, and charges against them were dropped. As his division was readied for moving to the European front, he introduced the concept of the value of Navajos' speaking a language that no one else could understand. The Navajo Code Talkers became critical to the battle that began in December.

Grateful for the warmth of his brother's naval coat—a coat that other soldiers much coveted—Shorts moved into the final stages of the war. The Battle of the Bulge, which began December 16, 1944, was the largest land battle of the war in which the United States participated. It pushed the weakened enemy to the east, but not before German jet planes flew overhead, releasing bombs. These planes were so much faster than the U.S. conventional P-38s and P-47s that they made the American planes seem as though they were standing still. The accuracy of the German jets, however, had not caught up with their speed, and they often missed their targets.

Shorts thinks he was one of the first Americans to cross the Elbe River, in April 1945, a milestone that marks the collapse of Germany's defenses.[13] Shorts's unit was the first of the Allies to reach a small labor camp, near Hanover. He remembers that it was a warm day and he saw a man in black and white stripes lying there. Shorts assumed the man was dead until a fly landed on the man's face and he blinked.

The troops entered a building with wooden bunks stacked four or five high, no mattresses, and only flimsy blankets. The prisoners were too weak to move. There was a large pit in the side yard, where the dead were tossed and covered with a thin layer of dirt. The survivors were treated by American medics. The Division Commander rounded up the townspeople, who watched the prisoners march through the town each morning on their way to work and back again at night, and the General made them come to the Labor Camp, walk through it, and look at the horror. They had simply closed their minds to the atrocities committed by the Nazis, and they registered shock at the degradation with which their Jewish countrymen were treated.

V–E Day in 1945 was followed by the Potsdam Conference outside Berlin. Harry Truman, Winston Churchill, and Joseph Stalin met from July 17 to August 2, with two major items on the agenda:

Partitioning of post-war Europe

Resolving problems in the Pacific

Halfway through this critical meeting of world leaders, Churchill was defeated in his reelection for Prime Minister and had to return immediately to London, leaving the other leaders and their staffs with unscheduled time in Potsdam.

The Chief-of-Staff to General Alexander Bolling at Weinheim was Colonel Louis H. Truman, a cousin of the President. The Colonel was Shorts's immediate superior in the 63rd. With a recess in the partitioning proceedings, President Truman decided to visit his cousin. Shorts was asked to be in charge of planning the presidential luncheon for about fourteen attendees. Among those seated were Truman, General Dwight D. Eisenhower, his naval aide Captain Harry C. Butcher, Secretary of State James F. Byrnes, Secretary of War Henry L. Stimson, and one secret serviceman.

As they were preparing to sit down, Shorts was asked to join them for lunch because the President did not want a secret serviceman at the table. Shorts knew the military's best guess as to how long it would take to complete the war in the Pacific was five years. Shorts remembers President Truman saying, "The war will be over by Christmas.... Oh, I shouldn't have said that." What Truman knew, and no one else at the table knew, was the existence of an atomic bomb.

Following the war, Shorts returned to his wife and daughters in Madison Park and lived there until 1997, when he moved to a retirement community.

SEATTLE'S CONTRIBUTIONS TO THE WAR

By 1941, Seattle's population had reached 360,000. Within a year of the outbreak of World War II, the city became important to the war effort in three areas: its port facilities, the shipyards, and airplane production. The Boeing Company first contributed the B-17, a Flying Fortress used in the European theater, which "could take a beating and still make it home."[14] The following year came the B-29 Superfortress with more capability for the war against Japan.

The years 1942–1945 were the only years that the ferries on Lake Washington realized a profit. The *Leschi* carried workers, employed at the Houghton shipyard on Lake, from Madison Park to Kirkland and back again. This Lake Washington facility, which employed as many as 6,000 workers, turned out sub-tenders and other small naval vessels destined for the South Pacific.

James Marshall remembers that as a teenager, he had a summer job as a riveter at the shipyard, which operated 24 hours a day, 7 days a week.[15] He and many other workers walked onto the ferry at Madison Park, got off 30 minutes later in Kirkland, and walked to Houghton. The afternoon ferry ride back to Seattle, Marshall recalls, was crowded with workers who stopped at one of the several taverns operating at Madison Park.

SUMMERS IN MADISON PARK

Douglas Fields remembers summers at Madison Park when he was a boy.[16] It might have been getting up at daybreak to hunt for coins and redeemable bottles along the beach. More lucrative and more fun was to be in the Lake, swimming and welcoming the ferry filled with shipyard workers as it came into the slip. Doug and other boys and girls chanted, "Penny, nickel, dime. Catch it every time." In response, the workers tossed coins to the children treading water below. As soon as the ferry pulled out for the return trip to Kirkland, the swimmers dived to the sandy lake bottom and used a tin can with holes punched in the bottom to retrieve any coins they missed during the toss. They swam until the next ferry approached and then began the chant again.

Mitzi Balkema lived on McGilvra Boulevard and attended McGilvra School.[17] She and her parents, Dr. James and Gertrude Carver Balkema, lived just south of the Tennis Club, and her grandmother, Florence Carver, owned three cottages on 43rd north of Madison. Mitzi remembers that when she was sleeping in one of the cottages, the whistle of the first ferry-run of the morning served as the alarm clock. She also remembers what fun it was to spend the night with the girl across the street, who lived in a houseboat. When the ferry arrived or left, it gently rocked the houseboat. She remembers, too, that the *The Seattle Times* offered free swim lessons for several summers at Madison Park.

Next door to Florence Carver on 43rd North was one of Mitzi's best friends, Ann Johnson. The girls were classmates at McGilvra School, Garfield High School, and the University of Washington. Ann's father, Michael C. Johnson, was in the real estate business and saw the value of maintaining the property at the foot of East Lynn Street as a park. The Hagans remember that he spent four or five years appealing to the State Legislature to keep the park as a green space.[18] As the neighborhood developed, it was an enhancement to the use of 43rd North and, still unnamed, might be known as Michael C. Johnson Park.

THE REED HOUSE FIRE AND BILL REED

In Madison Park on October 4, 1942, at approximately 4:15 a.m., 9-year-old Frank cried, "Fire!" which awakened the cook in her room at the far end of the Frank Cambell Reed house. She opened her bedroom door to find the hall full of smoke and flames. After kicking the screen out of her window, she dropped two stories to the ground and ran for help. The fire had started in the library—most likely from a cigarette's dropping into an overstuffed chair—directly under the boy's bedroom, where it smoldered and finally burst into flame.

The gate tender, who lived a short distance away, ran to the burning house while his wife called the Fire Department. He reached the second floor but heard no sound except the crackling of the flames. The smoke and flames forced him back. As he crawled down the stairs, he heard the sirens of the approaching fire rigs. The Fire Department extinguished the flames within a few minutes, but the Frank Reed family of five was dead from the terrible heat and smoke before the firemen reached the scene.

William (Bill) Reed, now himself the father of three young children, recalled that "they asked me to go upstairs to identify the bodies, and the firemen led me to where lay my brother, his wife, and all three of their children. To my horror, they had all been suffocated by smoke." [19] In an 18-month period, Bill lost his mother, grandmother, brother, sister-in-law, and nephews, "a succession of tragic events hard to believe and much harder to accept."

Bill Reed was in the Navy in 1942, and in November Vice-Admiral Frank Jack Fletcher became Commander of the 13th Naval District and Commander of the Northwestern Sea Frontier. Reed and Fletcher became friends, and the Admiral tapped Bill to be his aide at the naval station on Adak, in the Aleutian Islands.

LATER DAYS OF THE WAR—GEORGE POWELL AND JOHN RUPP

In his family history account, George Powell remembers that their nanny, originally from Conway, Washington, "came to us and said that she and her sister were going to work for Boeing. She said, "Boeing is getting very busy with defense work and needs to include women in the work force."[20]

When the war began, George and Katherine Powell had three young children. One of Powell's early contributions to the war effort was on the local ration board. He remembers that "a great many things were being rationed, that is, shoes, gasoline, meat, butter, sugar, etc. Regional ration boards were set up throughout the city to deal with requests for increased amounts of rationed items." Gasoline, for instance, was limited to three gallons a week for nonessential vehicles.

Powell was also a member of what was called an ambulance unit. "People were concerned after Pearl Harbor that Seattle might be subjected to some sort of attack. Various organizations of citizens were formed to deal with any such episode. One was groups of people with automobiles who were able and willing to act as de facto ambulances if the necessity arose."

He applied for a commission in the Navy and was called to active duty early in 1944. Following indoctrination in Tucson, P. K. Leberman, a friend of his sister Ah Lou, "put in a request for me which resulted in my going to Washington, D.C. to be under him in the Radio Division of the Bureau of Ships. Leberman, who was an Annapolis graduate in the Naval Reserve, had been ordered back into the Navy when the War started and before that had been operating a radio station in Seattle. My job was to be a contract negotiator for electronic gear for the Navy's vessels and aircraft. That included radio and the new Radar, Loran, Sonar, etc."

After some months, the Bureau of Ships was reorganized, which presented an opportunity for Powell to get back to the West Coast and his family. An old friend from Seattle, Stephen Moser, was in the Navy, stationed in Tacoma with the Supervisor of Shipbuilding at the Todd Shipyard. He put in a request for Powell, and the Captain in charge of all personnel with the Supervisors of Shipbuilding sent Powell to a month's course at the new Pentagon. Young officers had been brought in from all over the world to attend the school, mostly lawyers and accountants, from the Army, Navy, Marines and Air Force.

Congress had just passed the Contract Settlement Act, designed to prevent the long delays following the end of World War I. No matter how many dollars were involved or how much in materials, these young officers were to take full responsibility for removing the residues of war so a civilian economy could resume. A few days before the Japanese surrendered, the Navy in Washington canceled the Todd Shipyard contract to build escort carriers in Tacoma. That same day, with five carriers (CVEs) under construction, Powell gave the order, "Start cutting them up." Until that moment, "everyone had been working full tilt to further the war effort," and in a matter of a few hours, that was reversed. "In a very short time the whole shipyard was cleaned up."

In 1944, John N. Rupp, an attorney and naval officer, traveled to Tucson with George Powell for indoctrination. Following training in Arizona, Rupp received orders to go to Adak, first as a staff member of the 17th Naval District and later, like Bill Reed, as an aide to Vice-Admiral Frank Jack Fletcher.

Rupp wrote, "I think it fair to say that of all the wars waged by mankind, the Second World War was the most interesting. It went on for six years, and involved most of the world's nations, and was fought on land, on the sea, under the sea and in the air, in all the oceans and on all the continents except Antarctica. In equipment, strategy, tactics, and numbers of fighting men it was unique."[21]

Elizabeth Gastman Powell died at age 81, and her son George was elected as a representative to the Washington State Legislature from the 37th district in Seattle, serving in the 1947, 1949, and 1951 sessions. Charles Stokes, the first African–American legislator to be sent to Olympia, was his running mate in the 1949 election.

POST-WAR EXPANSION

In 1943 the Seattle city limits extended north to 145th Street. Residential development, like many other domestic industries, had slowed to almost nothing between 1929 and 1945. Housing construction began again in 1946 as men and women returned from their war-time assignments to their families. Those who had postponed marriage until after the war needed living quarters, too.

MADISON PARK MEMORIES: BERNIE HAGAN AND DOUG FIELDS

Bernard "Bernie" Hagan, who was born in Sioux City, Iowa, in 1922, was stationed with the Army at Fort Lawton, Seattle, in 1943. Through a series of circumstances, this enlisted man was billeted at the Olympic Hotel in Seattle, with orders to pick up supplies at the Port of Embarkation. While executing his duties, he met a young woman working there who had been a student at the University of Washington. Her name was Mitzi Balkema. Five days later Bernie proposed marriage and offered her a ring. Two years later, Bernie was discharged and back in the country. The two were married, settled in

Madison Park, and welcomed first Jim, then Nanette, Kim, and Tim, into their family. Bernie chose a career in commercial printing and publishing.[22]

At the Garfield High School graduation in June of 1944, all but two of the seniors were dressed in caps and gowns: Robert Fields and Robert Fletcher received their diplomas wearing U.S. Navy dress blues. Thirteen-year-old Doug Fields remembers both seamen receiving standing ovations from the packed auditorium moved by respect and patriotism.[23]

McGILVRA SCHOOL

At the end of the school year in the spring of 1948, the seventh grade of McGilvra School was photographed on the front steps. This was their last year at McGilvra, and most could remember Kindergarten with Bessie Dick Smith. In Room 1, Viola Caldwell taught 1B, and Lester R. Roblee was the school's Principal, in his last term at the school. Jeannette Nelson was the teacher for 1A and 2B.

For third grade, the class moved upstairs to Gertrude Meehan's room, and there was a new Principal, Mr. J. Bernard Chichester. Esther North and Ann Redlinger were the fourth grade teachers. Louise H. Noon taught 5B and was also the school's Art teacher. Faith Voorhees King taught 5A. Sixth grade was in the new wing with Lena M. Streams and Velma Foster, who was also the Music teacher. William A. Tucker taught Science and Physical Education.

By seventh grade there was another new Principal, Donald G. Olts. Elizabeth H. Austin, the school secretary, lived just a couple of blocks away with her two sons, Philip and Charles. Forrest E. and Vilma W. May, the school cook, also lived nearby and had three children attending McGilvra—Bruce, Wayne, and Dawn.

McGilvra School seventh grade poses on the front steps in June 1948. Photo by Perkins Studio.

Front Row; left to right: Gael Burns, Jo Ann Martin, Caroline Devereaux, Marlene Randall, Avonne Wilson, Ruth Udell, Patty Newman, Carol Jacobson, Carol Stigenwalt, Nancy Burgess

Second Row; left to right: Wayne May, David Correa, Gary Geiger, Raymond Allen, Ron Richardson, Fred Collins, Gilman Chase, Russell Hadfield, Leonard Mickelson

Third Row; left to right: Joan Walling, Patricia Helgason, Ginny Vining, Marie Braunschweiger, Donna Berthelson, Barbara Sloan, Mary Hoak, Bonnie Lee, Susie Wakefield

Back Row; left to right: Fred Willis, Jake Hausman, Scott Railton, Michael Gormley, Bob Lewis, Jack Morton, Eddie Tyler, Bill Fite, Don Davis

BOEING AND JAY MORRISON

In 1950, The Boeing Company named 63-year-old Jay Morrison manager of the company's gas turbine project. Morrison was a member of the Boeing executive staff in 1938, and 5 years later became vice-president and general manager of Boeing Aircraft of Canada, Ltd. Seattle directories show that in 1955 Morrison was living on Shenandoah Drive in Broadmoor. He remained there until shortly before his death in 1970.

Born in Omaha in 1887, Jay was 4 years older than his brother, Edward Morrison, who flew with 1st Lt. C.C. Moseley in 1923. Jay graduated from Phillips Academy in Andover, Massachusetts, in

McGilvra School patrol boys are shown on the front steps in 1947. Photo by Perkins Studio.

Front row, left to right: Tom Donnan, Lee Price, Taylor Scott, Bill Fite

Second row, left to right: Wayne May, Allen Monsen, Gilman Chase, Fred Collins, Gary Geiger, Russell Hadfield

Third row, left to right: Don Davis, Fred Willis, Bill Buchan, Arthur Stroud, unidentified, Paul Pickard

Top row, left to right: Scott Railton, Jim Douglas, unidentified, Bob Lewis, Skip Kachlein, Nat Dickinson

1907, and from Harvard University in 1911. Surviving correspondence indicates that when he was at Harvard, his family was living in Billings, Montana, raising cattle.

During his freshman year, Morrison applied for a scholarship with the following remarks: "The $650 which I can depend on for this year includes railroad fare from Montana to Boston, and so the amount left for use in Cambridge is considerably less, about $520. Owing to legal complications, some money upon which my father had been depending to pay my expenses is, at present, unavailable. This makes it necessary for me to do all in my power to aid." [24]

Morrison received a scholarship, which allowed him to complete two years before taking a year's leave of absence. He spent that year in Bonner, Montana, working in the Office of Engineer of the Big Blackfoot Railway Company. When he returned for his third and senior year, he was able to satisfy requirements for a Bachelor of Arts degree in Civil Engineering with Phi Beta Kappa distinction.

He became an instructor in Forest Surveying at Harvard for a year, and then moved to Seattle. In 1917, he enlisted in the Army and served with the 213th Engineers. Two years later he was discharged as 2nd Lieutenant of Engineers at Camp Lewis, Washington. Between 1925 and 1938, Morrison was employed by Washington Mutual Savings Bank, where his last position was that of Vice President. He also served as a member of the Advisory Board of Children's Orthopedic Hospital.

At age 61, Morrison bought a four-wheel-drive light truck and embarked on an adventure that no one had undertaken. He left Seattle on September 23, 1948, to drive a vehicle alone through every roadless country in South America—the hardest auto trip in the world—from Rio to Tierra del Fuega and north again through Colombia to Barranquilla. Upon his return, Boeing called Morrison to the gas turbine project.

CHAPTER 4

MADISON PARK BUSINESSES

COMMERCIAL VENTURES AT MADISON PARK in the late 1800s grew up as adjuncts to the amusement park promoted by John J. McGilvra. If families were going to visit these establishments on Sunday afternoons, promoters would have to offer activities and refreshments. Availability of the county's Land Use Survey photographs and release of the first Reverse Directory by Polk in 1938 facilitate a nostalgic look at Madison Park businesses.

At the head of the ferry pier on 43rd North was Riley's Confectionery Store. Walking south from the ferry dock along the promenade, the next establishments were Brown's Boat House, where Olive Baker McDougall remembers there was "a small replica of a steam locomotive,"[1] and the Cascade Canoe Club. Weather permitting, a popular pastime was to rent and paddle one of the many colorful canoes fitted with "lazy-backs" and cushions.

On 43rd Avenue North, Brown's Boat House continued in operation, and the owner was George E. Brown. At the head of the ferry dock, Jewett E. Riley owned Riley's Coffee Shop.

George Powell remembers the Katzenjammer Castle at the corner of 42nd and Madison, "named for the Katzenjammer kids, who were favorite comic strip characters at the time. The outside of the build-

Notice that the Ferry waiting room for foot passengers was through these doors on 43rd Avenue North. Courtesy of Washington State Archives–Puget Sound Regional Branch.

ing was made of metal molded to look like the stone work of which a castle was usually built. It stood for many years after the amusement park was no more."[2]

REST HAVEN

Just east of McGilvra Boulevard at 4009 East Madison Street, a one-and-a-half-story residence was built in 1905. Called Rest Haven, the exterior was frame and stucco on wood lath with a shingle roof. Inside there were 14 rooms with 10-foot ceilings and four bathrooms with claw-foot tubs. A wide veranda swept around the north and east sides of the main floor, with circle glass in two large windows. Early records show that Mrs. Lena Mason owned the rest home.

Later, Mrs. Aliene M. Cadigan was the owner. Doug Fields remembers that Mrs. Cadigan had a son, John Murray "Jack" Cadigan, who was a 1949 graduate of Seattle Prep.[3] Jack was born in Spokane and

Rest Haven is an impressive landmark at the entrance to the Madison Park business district. Courtesy of Washington State Archives–Puget Sound Regional Branch.

was stricken with polio as a boy, requiring him to use a wheelchair. He had many young friends in Madison Park and was affectionately called "The Pen" because of his ability to create credible fake I.D.s.

JOHN AND MILLIE JOHNSON'S HANDY GROCERY

Across Madison from Rest Haven stood the Handy Grocery, owned by John and Millie Johnson. Many Madison Park children remember that this mom-and-pop store was the place you could buy penny candy. The Johnsons lived above the store with their children until they were able to invest in a home on East McGilvra Street.

THE STOLLS AND THEIR BAKERY

At Seattle's German Club on Ninth Avenue, a 23-year-old man and a 21-year-old woman first met in 1923—more than 20 years before opening Stoll's Madison Park Bakery together. They had both recently arrived in the United States from Germany, he from Brittheim and she from Eichstetten. Herman Stoll was one of the younger children of a man who was both a tailor and a farmer in Germany. Elsie was one of several children from a farming family.

Herman Stoll is shown at the entrance to his Bakery with Madison Park resident Lynn Hammond. Courtesy of *The Seattle Times.*

Sponsors were a necessary part of the immigration process. Herman had a cousin in the construction business living in Seattle, so Herman spent his first few years in Seattle in the building trades. He first became a baker at Jersey Cream, then at the Rotary Bakery in the Pike Place Market. As her sponsor, Elsie had an uncle in Seattle who owned a delicatessen at 19th and Union, where she worked for a couple of years after coming to the United States. Before World War II, Germany was suffering from a Depression, and Herman sponsored two of his brothers coming to New York. Elsie, too, sponsored the immigration of two of her brothers—one a painter and the other a baker.

Herman and Elsie were married in 1926 at the First German Congregational Church at 11th and Howell. As the years passed, they had four children—Walt, Trudy, Fred, and Marlene. In January 1945, the Stolls bought the bakery in Madison Park, where they and all of their children worked. In 1966, son Fred and his wife Nancy bought the bakery from his parents and continued the tradition of delicious goods and many friendships in the neighborhood.

HADFIELDS' GARAGE

One of the oldest Union Oil dealers in the Pacific Northwest opened a garage in Madison Park in 1924 and built a house next door. Born in Iowa, Abner F. "Slim" Hadfield married Mable C. Allison in 1904, and they and their first son came West, where they homesteaded on the Olympic Peninsula and he worked as a logger near Blyn. The Hadfields' next home was on Vashon Island, before they came to Madison Park in 1917 with four young sons.

There, Slim began working as an auto mechanic, reasoning that anyone venturing all the way to Madison Park in an automobile would most likely need the services of a mechanic in order to return home. The Hadfields soon welcomed a daughter and, in 1919, their

Slim Hadfield is pictured in front of his Madison Park Garage. Courtesy of the Hadfield family.

Slim's sons, Rex, Bud, Bus and Howard Hadfield, apprenticed and then operated the garage. Photo by Marilyn Warner.

sixth child, a boy. All of the Hadfield children were students at the J. J. McGilvra School. Mitzi Hagan remembers that her father, Dr. Balkema, was the first customer at Slim's Madison Park Garage. Mitzi attended Sunday School classes taught by Mrs. Hadfield in Pioneer Hall.[4]

When Ross "Bus" Hadfield was attending McGilvra, one of his school friends was Albert Dissel, Jr. Albert had a younger sister, Marie, who also went to McGilvra. The years passed, and eventually Bus and Marie were married. The couple stayed in Madison Park and raised a family there. Russell was their firstborn in 1935, followed by Forrest, Mark, Marty, and Roxanne. All of these Hadfield children attended McGilvra, too. Records show that Bus and Marie were the first J. J. McGilvra graduates to marry, whose children were schooled at their parents' elementary school.

A neighbor of the Hadfields, Marilyn Warner, photographed and wrote an article about them for the *The Seattle Times* in 1973.[5] After World War II, four of the Hadfield brothers—Howard, Ross "Bus," Rex, and Clair "Bud"—worked side by side at the garage.

THE BUCHANS—FISHING, HOME BUILDING, AND SAILING

In 1924, a 49-year-old Scottish fisherman, his wife Elizabeth, and two of their four children arrived in Boston and crossed the continent by train to Seattle. They had left home in Peterhead, Scotland, on the maiden voyage of Cunard Line's *Mesopotamia*.[6] The William Buchan family began a new life in America. The younger of the two boys, 21-year-old William, and his older brother John had already left for Southeastern Alaska to fish for herring. Their parents and two sisters joined the boys outside Ketchikan that summer.

Just two years after arriving in America, William Sr. died shortly after having surgery in Seattle. The family thinks his illness might have resulted from a head injury incurred years earlier in a fall aboard a sailing fish boat. Elizabeth and her four children remained in Seattle, picking up the pieces of their lives and making a new home. William and John, together with their mother, opened the Post Office Fish Market at 3rd and Union in downtown Seattle. Shortly afterward, John died while vacationing in British Columbia, leaving William with a mother and two much younger sisters to support.

Irene M. Johnsen was born in Duluth, Minnesota, in 1911 and came to Washington as a 4–year-old with her widowed mother and 6-year-old brother, Elmer. One evening, when Irene was in her early 20s, she was with her friend, Gertrude Kruger, at the Trianon Ballroom in Seattle. That evening she met William Buchan, and they danced. They were married in 1933. Their first child, Bill, was born in 1935, and the family settled in Madison Park. A second son, John, and a daughter, Linda, completed the family. While owning and running the fish business, William began building homes and boats.

William Buchan Homes, founded in 1960, and John Buchan Construction, founded a few years later, carried on the family's building tradition that began in Madison Park years earlier. In 1947, the Buchans bought the property north of the Shoremont Apartments on 43rd Avenue North, which the family developed into the Buchan Apartments, owned by Bill and John's families to this day.

Castle Dye Works fits comfortably in the building that was known in earlier years as the Katzenjammer Castle. Courtesy of Washington State Archives–Puget Sound Regional Branch.

Bill Buchan reports that, in his spare time, his father built a variety of sailboats for himself over the years.[7] In the summer of 1948, 13-year-old Bill had just finished the seventh grade at McGilvra School and Seattle was hosting the North American Championship for Star sailboats. He watched the boats racing on Shilshole Bay and decided he wanted one. His father suggested that they build it themselves. The winter storage place for the Puget Sound Star Fleet of about 20 boats was the Hadfields' Garage in Madison Park. It was convenient for father and son to go to the garage to pick up ideas for the construction of the boat. *Torrid* was completed and certified in 1949.

Bill recounts that his brother John was in business with their father, building 40- foot sailboats in the basement of the Washington Pioneer Hall on 43rd Avenue North. This was the beginning of what would become the Buchan Boat Company. The company and its family of sailors came to be known worldwide.

In the 1950s, William sold the fish market he had owned for 25 years so he could pursue his life's dream of becoming a commercial fisherman. Son Bill continued working through high school for the new owner of the fish market. After an unsuccessful experience as a fisherman, building boats became William's vocation, not just a hobby. He designed and built more than 50 of the Buchan 37 class of sailboats, many of which are still racing and cruising the waters of the Pacific Northwest.

The Mallory Cup, commonly referred to as the North American Men's Sailing Championship, was held in Detroit in 1955. The winning boat was skippered by 20-year-old Bill, with his father and a friend, Ron McFarlane, as crew.

APARTMENTS AND ARCHITECTS—
WILLIAM BAIN, PAUL THIRY, AND JOHN GRAHAM, SR.

The first apartment complex in Madison Park, the Shoremont Apartments, was built in 1926 just north of the ferry dock and on Lake Washington. Duane Dietz wrote that "the French Provincial mode is represented at the Shoremont Apartments."[8] The owner was William Duxor, and the architect was William James Bain, Sr., just 30 years old when he designed this landmark. In 1928, Bain won an honor from the Washington State Chapter of the American Institute of Architects for this project.[9]

Bain was born in 1896 in New Westminster, British Columbia, and moved with his family to Seattle when he was 8 years old. He attended Broadway High School and knew then that he wanted to become an architect. He apprenticed with both W. R. B. Willcox and Arthur L. Loveless before enlisting in the Army when the United States entered World War I. After serving in France, he wrote, "I had decided to attend architectural school at the University of Pennsylvania, which was offering a special class for ex-servicemen with previous experience in architecture."[10] Bain graduated in 1921, and "worked briefly again for Willcox and for Loveless, before opening his own office in Seattle in 1924."[11]

Immediately south of the Shoremont Apartments was an adjoining piece of property that owner William Duxor wished to develop in 1928. In an interview with Meredith L. Clausen for the Smithsonian, Architect Paul Albert Thiry remembered that "I started practice before I finished the University, because I lived in the Shoremont Apartments on the Lake, and the owner of the building was going to build another apartment next door called the Lakecrest and so he asked me to design it. William Duxor, the owner, commissioned me to be the architect.... He wanted a similar Normandy-style apartment."[12]

Thiry was born in 1904 in Nome, Alaska, of French parents. After 2 years, the family left the Arctic and settled in San Francisco just in time to experience the devastating 1906 earthquake. At the urging of Paul's mother, the Thirys returned to Paris for a time, until Paul's father, Georges, again prevailed and they returned to Nome. With the outbreak of World War I in Europe in 1914, the elder Thiry enlisted in the French Corps, went to war, and didn't return.

His widow and their son Paul moved to Seattle, where she placed an advertisement in the city directory: "Importer, Designer of Artistic Gowns, Trousseaux a Specialty, Models from Leading Couturiers of Paris." Paul was enrolled at St. Martin's preparatory school near Olympia and graduated at age 15. At his mother's urging, he entered the University of Washington to study medicine, but the only classes that appealed to him were in anatomical drawing.

The founder and head of the Department of Architecture was Carl Freylinghausen Gould, also a friend of Mme. Louise Thiry. With Gould's encouragement, Paul switched to architecture, which permitted him 3 months of study at L'Ecole des Beaux Arts in Fontainebleau before he graduated in 1928. Clausen wrote that the Lakecrest Apartment "presents a picturesque composition with motifs and details from French provincial sources."[13]

The Edgewater Apartments opened in January 1939 with 316 one- and two- bedroom units. The apartments were designed in a traditional manner, in two-story buildings. Interior courtyards with grass and trees, and some apartments with views to the Lake, compliment the interior design details and over the years have made this a sought-after residence for young and old alike.

The original owner of the Edgewater Apartments was an entity called the Madison Park Corporation. Public records show that officers of this corporation were the son of the project's architect, John Graham, Jr. and William L. Painter, a partner of John Graham, Sr. and an engineer. The two founding members were O. Albert Carlson, President–Treasurer of O.A. Carlson Electric Company, and Arvid Strand, Secretary–Treasurer of Henrikson–Alstrom Construction. The two other officers of the Madison Park Corporation were Clark R. Jackson of Hiawatha Pharmacy and State Director of the Federal Housing Administration, and Frank O. Granston, President of Northwest Distilleries, Inc. and of University Plumbing and Heating Company, Inc

John Graham Sr., was a significant contributor to the architecture of Madison Park and Seattle. By the time he was 66, his firm had become one of Seattle's largest corporate architectural practices. Grant Hildebrand wrote, "His career embraced a great variety of building types in many styles, including a large number of Seattle's major urban commercial buildings."[14] Among those cited in Hildebrand's essay were the Frederick & Nelson, the Dexter Horton, and the Exchange buildings.

THE CROSHAWS AND THEIR GROCERY BUSINESS

For a short time, Thomas Bert Croshaw and his wife Lucille managed the United Grocers store and lived in Madison Park. In 1932, they opened their first grocery store, Bert's Pay Day Foods, at 4200 East Madison Street. In an interview many years later, Croshaw reminisced that, "customers would come in with their lists, and we would fill their orders for them by running through the aisles, pulling down the items they wanted, and carrying it all back up front in our aprons."[15] Fourteen years after its inception, the grocery store moved, and Bert's IGA opened a block away at 41st and Madison. The

Bert Croshaw, on one of his Palomino horses, carries the flag in a parade. Photo by Dorothy P. Frick.

Croshaw family continues to own and serve the community at the store today.

Bert was one of 11 children born to a family in the small town of Oxford, Idaho, in 1907. He wrote, "We lived on a 160 acre ranch about 5 or 6 miles from town, my dad was a devoted farmer; cows, horses, chickens, pigs. We grew hay, oats, barley, fall wheat and spring wheat."[16] He went on to say, "Of the four boys, I was the second and I always liked to be with my dad. He was a real lover of horses and always had the best saddle horse in town. My dad always saw that we boys had a good pony."

His wife Lucille was from the same Idaho valley, from a family of seven children. After the two married, they moved to Kent, Washington, where Bert was a grocery store manager. He praised his wife, saying, "Lucille helped me a lot and has been a great help mate ever since." They had two children, Roger Paul and Berta Lou. Both Bert and Lucille became accomplished horseback riders and enjoyed a cattle ranch in Ellensburg for 17 years. Progress, in the form of an interstate highway through the ranch, brought them to Cottage Lake, and a smaller place for their four Palomino horses.

Lucille Croshaw marches in a parade on one of her Palomino horses. Photo by Dorothy P. Frick.

THE LINDLEYS AND THEIR DRUG STORE

Kenneth J. Lindley, born in Seattle in 1906, was raised in Centralia and graduated from the School of Pharmacy at Washington State College in 1926. In an interview upon his retirement, he said, "I got out of school at just the right time. The Depression hadn't started yet, but you could feel it coming."[17] He went to Oswego, Oregon, and was working for a druggist when he was reintroduced to Clara Zufafern, whom he had met 3 years earlier in Chehalis. In 1934, they were married and headed north to Seattle with the idea of settling down.

"A wholesale druggist told me," he said, "about a place called Cunningham Drugs down in Madison Park that was for sale. The owner had passed away and his widow was running the store. I went down and took a look. It was love at first sight. Not the drugstore. The Park. It was the most beautiful thing I had ever imagined. I asked Mrs. Cunningham if she wanted to sell and she said yes. That was 35 years ago and I wouldn't change a thing. All the store had then was a soda fountain. My wife would cook up a special chocolate sauce at home and we made sodas and sundaes. Actually I was a darn good soda

Cunningham Drugs, next door to the Castle Dye Works, was bought by Ken Lindley in the 1930s. Courtesy of Washington State Archives-Puget Sound Regional Branch.

Ken Lindley appears outside his pharmacy at 4200 East Madison Street. Photo by Dorothy P. Frick.

jerk." Ken owned the Madison Park Pharmacy at 4210 East Madison and in 1953 moved his store to the corner, 4200 East Madison.

Ken and Clara had no children, but in a very real sense, he loved all of the neighborhood children. Don Plumlee remembers Ken's generosity to his employees as well.[18] When Clara's brother Harry returned from New Guinea at the end of World War II, Ken paid his tuition at Pharmacy School and set Harry up in business in Magnolia. In August 1966, the Madison Park community had a parade and declared it Ken Lindley Day to honor this fine citizen.

VETERINARIANS IN MADISON PARK

Dr. Edward A. Schmoker opened Broadmoor Veterinary Hospital in 1939. Following WWII, Dr. Donald Anderson bought the practice on 43rd Avenue North, just north of the ferry dock, where he and his staff cared for pets until 1963.

ALONG MADISON STREET IN 1938

Walking west on Madison in the 4200 block in 1938, on the north side one would see the Safeway, Samuel Jaffe's Shoe Repair, Joseph B. Beriault's Barber Shop, and Betty's Quality Café with a wood-burning stove. Mrs. Georgia C. Stephens owned the Five and Ten Cent Store and lived on 41st Avenue North. The site of the original Red Onion was 4222 Madison, with A.B. Carver pulling beers and Beth Oakson in charge of food. Next came Madison Park Meats, with Guy

Terry as the butcher. Like several of the merchants, Guy worked and lived in Madison Park. The VandeKamps Holland Dutch Bakery was next.

There was a Ben Franklin Thrift Store, and then Eba's Mutual Grocery, with Frank F. Frick as the butcher. Earl Eba's father Herman had been a grocer in the Pike Place Market and a partner of Mr. Augustine (formerly of Augustine & Kyer). Benjamin Opperman had the second neighborhood bakery, and the last business on the block was Castle Cleaners, owned by George A. Wiseman. There are still reminders of the old Katzenjammer Castle in this building on East Madison Street.

BUD AND LOLA McKEE'S HARDWARE STORE

Immediately following World War II, a young woman who was a civilian employee of the United States Air Force arrived in Seattle. Lola Maitland was born in Parker's Prairie, Minnesota, and grew up on a farm. Her first assignment on the way west was in Salt Lake City. Then the Air Force transferred her and a friend to Alaska. The other woman got homesick and opted out.

H&H (Hardware and House Wares) Hardware became a landmark on 42nd Avenue East. Courtesy: Washington State Archives-Puget Sound Regional Branch.

Lola McKee is seen inside her Madison Park Hardware store. Courtesy of Lola McKee.

Alone in Seattle, Lola joined the ranks of many returning young servicemen and servicewomen looking for jobs and places to live. She found a position with the Seattle Fire Department as a stenographer by day, and on nights and weekends she worked at the Seattle Public Library in the University district.

One Friday night a young veteran, a Seattle native, came to the Library looking for a book on electricity, and the two met. Eight days later they had a marriage license, and the following Saturday Lola married Earle S. "Bud" McKee.

The McKees bought their first home in Madison Park on East Galer Street. Before long the family included two children, Jane and Scott, and the McKees were looking for a house that would be more comfortable for a family of five. In 1953 they moved to a house on 41st Avenue North, and daughter Jeri was born.

Nearby, the owner of H & H Hardware, Les Willits, wanted to make a trip to Florida. Having had bad experiences with dishonest clerks over the years, he asked Bud and Lola if they would cover for him while he was away. The McKees agreed to help him out, and they hired a nanny to oversee things at home. Soon after that, Willits decided to sell the hardware store and negotiated with Bud and Lola for them to continue to work for 2 more years until they could save for a down payment on the store. Lola remembers that she had live-in help while she worked 10 to 4, and that Bud came home for lunch.[19] In 1956, the McKees became the fourth owners of what is known today as the Madison Park Hardware.

CLOTHING STORES: RUTH TRIMBLE
AND HANNAHBETH STERN

The Pied Piper children's shop opened in 1948. New to Seattle, the owner was Ruth Kelly Trimble from Shreveport, Louisiana. Born in Austin, Texas, in 1915, she graduated from Texas Women's University, where she majored in Journalism and Home Economics. A single parent, she arrived in Seattle with her 8-year-old daughter Susan and 5-year-old son Robert. Before long, Ruth's mother, Erma Kelly, a recent widow, followed the

Ruth Trimble is pictured on vacation from her Madison Park shop. Courtesy of Susan Trimble Svenson.

family from Shreveport to Seattle and often helped in the shop. Ruth's daughter Susan remembers that her mother and Ken Lindley worked together to beautify the shopping district with planters and flowers.[20]

Madison Park welcomed the Stern family from Boston in 1946. Hannahbeth was born in Seattle in 1911, the daughter of Coral and Sol Spring. She graduated from Broadway High School, then left for Simmons College in Boston. The Spring family owned a Wholesale Cigar Company in Seattle for many years. While in Boston, Hannahbeth met, then married, Israel Stern, in 1933. The Sterns welcomed three daughters, Roseanne, Myrna, and Corie. When Corie was just 1 year old, the family moved to East McGilvra Street and lived in a guest house on the Spring grandparents' property.

The girls remember walking on a dirt road from home south to McGilvra School. Roseanne's class was the last eighth grade at McGilvra, and the last ninth grade at Garfield.[21] The following year

Hannahbeth Stern and an employee are pictured outside her Pied Piper Shop. Photo by Dorothy P. Frick.

marked the advent of junior high schools in Seattle, and Madison Park students were assigned to Edmond Meany.

When the girls were of school age, Hannahbeth worked for Anne Itkin in the Loveless Building on East Roy Street. She and Israel bought the Pied Piper from Ruth Trimble in 1959 and ran the children's shop for 10 years.

ALONG MADISON STREET IN 1948

Taking a stroll in 1948 from 43rd Avenue North, west along Madison, several changes were noticeable from a decade earlier. First on the block was a beer parlor, the Purple Poodle Tavern. Bert Croshaw's cousin Clifford Hatch was the grocer at Safeway. Abraham Jaffe was now the owner of the shoe repair store.

New owner of the Hollywood Barber Shop, with its red and white pole outside, was the Marsh family. The barber shop drew men and boys from Madison Park and beyond. Al Fontes oversaw the first chair, while his brother-in-law, Guy W. "Bill" Marsh, Jr., cut hair at the second chair and his father-in-law Guy W. Marsh maintained the last chair. The Marsh men lived in Madison Park, where Guy, Sr. was married to Lillie and Bill married Patricia.

Red and White Grocery and Meats, with Mr. Barnhart at the helm, replaced the Ben Franklin Thrift Store at 4218 Madison. Stoll's Madison Park Bakery was now the only bakery, and D'Litha's Beauty Salon was next door at 4212 Madison. Ken Lindley's name replaced Cunningham's at the Pharmacy, and John G. Heise was the owner of H & H Hardware across 42nd Avenue North.

Arthur B. Ackerman, his wife Irene, and the older two of their four children, Artie and Arlene, moved to Madison Park in 1951. Art was born in High Point, Washington, a small town east of Issaquah, in 1917, and Irene was born in Seattle. Long before becoming the neighborhood mail carrier, Art worked for Pacific Coast Forge, a steel company on Spokane Street. Like so many of his generation, he served in the United States Army, for 4 years. Art remembers those years as his being in four "foreign" countries: 1942 in the Louisiana swamps, 1943 in England, 1944 in France, and 1945 in the Philippines.[22] Upon his return to Seattle following the war, Art's sister introduced him to Irene, and the two were married in 1946. When they were settled in their house on East Garfield Street, Kathy and Brian were born.

Art Ackerman. Photo by Dorothy P. Frick.

After the neighborhood mail carrier, William Kneebone, retired in 1959, Art took over his route. Art remembers that Charles Parsons carried the Edgewater Apartments section and Mac Shoji, a veteran of the 442nd Regimental Combat Team, carried the mail for the business district. They all retired at about the same time in 1977.

ALONG MADISON STREET IN 1953

By 1953, the 43rd corner shop became Madison Park Grocers and Herb's Meats. The meat market had sawdust on the floor, and the butcher was Herb Nyquist, who lived nearby. For many years the store offered home delivery service to customers.

Just east of Stoll's Bakery, a women's apparel shop, called L. Marie, Inc., opened. A woman named Leola owned a beauty salon on the other side of the bakery. At 4210 Madison, where the pharmacy was for many years, the Bamboo Terrace, a Chinese restaurant, opened. Ken Lindley's Pharmacy was now on the corner beyond the Pied Piper, where Bert's Grocery had been for many years.

CHAPTER 5

MADISON PARK HOMES

HOMES IN MADISON PARK over the years have ranged from cottages and houseboats to family houses and stately homes, some designed by premier architects of the time. Here is a "print and photographic tour" of houses that contribute significantly to the Madison Park we know today.

THE OLDEST HOUSE REMAINING IN MADISON PARK, THE MEEKER VICTORIAN

Ezra Morgan Meeker was born in Huntsville, Ohio, in 1830. When he was 21 years old, he married his childhood sweetheart, Eliza Jane Sumner, of Marion County, Indiana. The young couple traveled to Iowa by ox-team to stake out a farm. Their first winter there was so severe that the Meekers, along with their infant son Marion, decided to join the thousands moving west on the Oregon Trail in 1852. Ezra Meeker eventually became a leading citizen of the Washington Territory and was known especially for his respectful treatment of Native Americans.

Olive Baker McDougall remembers that Ezra Meeker visited the school with a covered wagon and oxen,[1] telling the students of the many adventures on his and Eliza's first crossing of the continent, and

The Meeker house was moved before, then altered after this photo was taken. Photo courtesy of Washington State Archives–Puget Sound Regional Branch.

of his much later crossing at the age of 76. Ezra became passionate about saving the Oregon Trail. He gave speeches, raised money, and left monuments as he retraced the route of the resolute pioneers.

In 1893, Ezra Meeker built the house—believed to be the oldest house still standing in Madison Park—for his 31-year-old son Fred Sumner Meeker, and his wife, Clara Misamore Meeker. The three-story Victorian shingle house was moved in 1908 from its original site about half a block to the north of where it stands now. The Permit to Move exists today in the archives of the Department of Construction and Land Use.

GEORGE WRIGHT'S SHINGLE HOUSE

George E. Wright was a distinguished member of the Bar and a distinguished citizen, according to author Aubrey Haines.[2] He was born in Brookline, New Hampshire, in 1867, and graduated Phi Beta Kappa before studying law. Wright and his brother, William H., were both first listed in an 1893–94 Seattle directory. George began the practice of law and also established a business interest with William, called Wright Bros. In July of 1894 Wright was a member of the largest climbing party, numbering 14, that had reached the summit of Mt. Rainier. The party was led by Major Ingraham.

In 1895, Wright married Mary Estelle Wyckoff, a daughter of A. B. Wyckoff, the first commandant of the Puget Sound Navy Yard. The Wrights built the two-story shingle house the following year, and later had two daughters, Mary and Anna.

The granite hitching post shown in the photo still stands there today. Another remnant of the late nineteenth century remains in the garage: two horse stalls and, in the carriage house above, a now-covered opening through which hay was tossed. Wright served as president of several organizations—the Public Library Board of Seattle, the Municipal League, the Seattle Bar Association, and the Harvard Club.

Wright was a charter member and founder of the Seattle Mountaineers in 1907. A Mountaineer publication noted, "About a year ago, George E. Wright succeeded in interesting Stephen T. Miller, assistant to the Secretary of the Interior, in the erection of a shelter

The Wright house has been altered. Photo courtesy of Jean English Jones.

hut at Camp Muir on Mt. Rainier. The hut has now been completed, following plans drawn by Carl F. Gould, a member of the Mountaineers. The hut, measuring 8 by 20 feet, 7½ feet high, with three foot thick walls, was built during the summer under the direction of Eugene Frank, using lime and cement carried to the site on the backs of burros. The cost was $555."[3]

THE POWELLS' DUTCH COLONIAL HOUSE, AND ARCHITECT KIRTLAND KELSEY CUTTER

The Dutch Colonial house built in 1902 by John and Elizabeth Powell was designed by Kirtland Kelsey Cutter. According to George Powell, it had "a full basement plus three stories. There were four bedrooms on the second floor and two bedrooms on the third floor. A driveway made a complete circle around the house, so that one exited to the street at the same place one entered. The house originally had a coal furnace and I can remember the family taking delivery of 20 tons of coal at one time to be stored in the basement. Delivery was made at the back of the house. In the early 20's the method of heating was changed to an oil burner and I think that was probably when the driveway was changed."[4]

The Powell house has been altered. Photo courtesy of Washington State Archives–Puget Sound Regional Branch.

Architect Cutter, according to Henry Matthews, was born in 1860 in East Rockport, Ohio. He studied as an illustrator in New York and in Europe before deciding to become an architect. At age 26, Cutter moved to Spokane, where, despite his lack of architectural training, he soon received commissions, and even more work following Spokane's 1889 fire.[5] Matthews wrote that Cutter and Karl Gunnar Malmgren formed a partnership in 1893 and "built their reputation on impressive mansions. Cutter's early Seattle commissions represent his Shingle Style phase."

THE SPICKARD PROPERTY HOUSES AND ARCHITECT WILLIAM BAIN, SR.

A cottage with cedar siding and a cobblestone fireplace and chimney was built in 1905 on a Lakefront lot. When the water level of Lake Washington was lowered in 1917, the cottage was no longer at the water's edge. In 1937, Dr. Vernon Warren Spickard, who had been treating young patients at Children's Orthopedic Hospital on Queen Anne Hill for 15 years, bought the cottage. He wanted to bring his

The Spickard house has been moved from its original location. Photo courtesy of Washington State Archives–Puget Sound Regional Branch.

parents, William and Florence Spickard, to Seattle from Iowa and thought the one-and-a-half-story home on pier blocks in Madison Park would be suitable for them.

Spickard, born in Iowa in 1892, graduated from the University of Iowa and from the University of Pennsylvania Medical School, in 1918. He interned in Philadelphia and completed his residency at the Universities of Berlin and Vienna. He came to Seattle in 1919 and joined the staff of Children's Orthopedic Hospital on Queen Anne Hill in 1923.

Later he became Chief of Staff, and held that position from 1952 until 1967, through the hospital's move to its present site in Laurelhurst.

His wife, Mildred Beim Spickard, also was born in Iowa, and she attended Drake University. The Spickards had two sons, Warren Beim and Donald Eliott. When the boys were young, the family lived on Queen Anne Hill and also had a summer home on Mercer Island when there was still ferry service from the island to Leschi. If the doctor responded to a house call and the ferry was not running, one of the boys took the doctor to the Leschi landing in a small boat.

On the Spickard property in Madison Park, stretching from the old cottage, where he installed his parents, to the new shoreline, Dr. Spickard and his wife built a new house in 1941. Of local interest is a document showing that in 1908 residents were granted a petition to vacate 42nd Avenue North for one block between East Lee Street and East Highland Drive. The Spickard property was one of the beneficiaries of this petition.

Emilie Schwabacher wrote, "As much as any single individual, Vern Spickard was responsible for the establishment of the University of Washington Medical School after World War II. He always felt that medical education and research were necessary to maintain the quality of medical care in a community. Dr. Spickard has had a profound influence on the medical community of Seattle.... Modest and retiring, he chose to accomplish the most effective leadership by example, guiding others to their potential through his own great ability.... Dr.

Spickard's influence on pediatrics as it is currently practiced in this community, and on the standard of care given to children at COH, is greater that any other living person."[6]

For their new home on Lake Washington, on the property that had been under water 25 years earlier, the Spickards commissioned architect William J. Bain, Sr. He wrote, "I was doing mostly residential work then and in fact had the largest residential office in the state." [7]

The Spickard house has been altered. Photo courtesy of Washington State Archives–Puget Sound Regional Branch.

At the entrance to the garden stands a statue called Boy with a Fish, sculpted for the Spickards by neighbor Dudley Pratt. Features of the house include Philippine mahogany paneling in the den and in both the living room and dining room bay windows. The terrace, accessible from the principal rooms, leads out onto a large lawn and to the lakeshore, where the dock and boat house are located.

The Spickards' elder son Warren graduated from Stanford undergraduate and medical schools and married Josephine McColl in 1941. The young couple lived in the Spickard cottage from 1944 to 1946, although Warren was away much of that time during World War II. The family outgrew the house (eventually there were five children) and moved to Mercer Island.

This Spickard house has been altered. Photo courtesy of Washington State Archives–Puget Sound Regional Branch.

Younger brother Donald also graduated from Stanford and the University of Washington Law School. He and his wife, Mary Alice Adkins, had two sons and, by 1950, wanted to stay in Madison Park. Rather than tear down the cottage that the Spickard families had outgrown, they sold it, and it was barged to the south end of Mercer Island.

Returning to the Spickard lot on 42nd Avenue North, vacant with the removal of the cottage, Donald and Mary Alice built a one-story house with a one-half basement in 1950. Features of this house are an entry hall, surprisingly large living room, large picture windows, and hardwood floors Once again, the family asked William Bain, Sr. to design this home to accommodate a family of four.

According to author Duane Dietz, Bain served as Washington State AIA chapter president from 1941 to 1943.[8] He was elected a Fellow of the AIA in 1947. That same year, he formed a partnership with Harrison Overturf, which enabled him to maintain a residential practice separate from the Naramore, Bain, Brady and Johanson partnership. Following World War II, there was a "new Modern approach to residential design on the West Coast," which this house exemplifies.

THE HYDE HOUSE AND ARCHITECTS BEBB AND MENDEL

Madison Park's most important home architecturally was featured in the 1913 book, *Homes and Gardens of the Pacific Coast.* It was described in the following manner: "The lofty four-columned Corinthian portico stands in charming contrast to the red brick of the main part of the house."[9] It was built on one-half acre by Samuel Hyde between 1908 and 1910.

Hyde was born in South Stafford, England, in 1858, and migrated to Pennsylvania as a 21-year-old. There he worked as a coal miner before coming to Seattle in 1888, a year before Washington became a state. He became involved in a coal mining venture in Cumberland and eventually owned the Hyde Mines there, which were later sold to the Pacific Coast Coal Company. Before Prohibition, Hyde also owned and managed the Hyde Liquor Company. He married Rachel, and they had three children, George S., Claire, and Mildred.

Years later, his daughter, Claire Hyde Jones, by then married, wrote, "I still have pictures of many of the rooms with all the large statuary and heavy furniture. The garage was used first as a carriage house. My father bought us a seven passenger Stevens Duryea touring car right away and a limousine a short time later. We had a gas tank

The Hyde house has been altered. Photo courtesy of Washington State Archives–Puget Sound Regional Branch.

near the garage, as I don't think there were service stations in those days. The apartment over the garage was meant for our chauffer, but was never occupied by him as he had quite a large family."[10]

In a later letter, Claire remembered, "Of course there was no radio then, so when they had a little dance, they would have a small orchestra."[11] Newspaper coverage of one dinner party at the Hyde house mentions that "Wagner's orchestra" furnished the music during dinner, after which "the guests adjourned to the ball room, where dancing was indulged in until a late hour."[12]

Claire remembers an efficient intercom system that allowed her mother to talk to the kitchen or to the garage from the master bedroom. "There was a turn table in the garage, which made it easy to get the car in and out." [13]

The architects for this landmark house were Charles Herbert Bebb and Louis Leonard Mendel. David Rash and Dennis Anderson wrote that by the end of the 1890s, the firm these architects established became the most prominent architectural practice in Seattle during the first decade and a half of the twentieth century.[14]

Bebb was born at West Hall, Mortlake, Surrey, England in 1856, and was educated at a preparatory school in Switzerland before attending the University of Lausanne. Back in London, he studied civil engineering at the School of Mines. He came to Seattle in 1893 as an architectural engineer for the Denny Clay Company, and five years later opened his own office as an architect.

Mendel was born in Mayen, Germany, and came to the United States in 1882, when he was 15 years old. Having worked for noted architectural firms across the country, by 1899 he "appears to have worked as a draftsman for Charles Bebb. By February 1901, Bebb and Mendel formed a partnership, which would last for 13 years and result in some of Seattle's largest and finest homes, hotels and businesses buildings."[15] Businessman Samuel Hyde, for whom money was no object, must have admired the nearby house designed in 1906–07 for William Walker by Bebb and Mendel.

Dorothy Brant Brazier wrote an article about the Hyde house, describing a large stained glass window above the stair landing made in Italy, which "faithfully reproduces the view from the front door."[16] Rooms on the main floor include a 12 x 24 foot entry hall, a larger living room, music room, dining room, breakfast room, and kitchen. There were front and back staircases. All of the canvas ceilings in the house were painted in Europe and sent over for installation when the house was built".

Claire Hyde Jones wrote that "all the rugs were from Austria and took over a year to make. Frederick & Nelson loaned us rugs until we received ours."[17] It seems fitting that the grand house of Samuel Hyde also had a garden designed by the Olmsted Brothers of Boston.

THE DISSEL HOUSE AND CARL BRICKEN

Albert Dissel came to Seattle as a young man. Born in Philadelphia in 1878, he came west looking for work. Anna Gasslein, also born in Philadelphia, came to Seattle to join an older sister living here. Albert and Anna met here and married. Early in his career, Dissel was a salesman for Realty Associates of Seattle and, later, for T. L. Blood Co.,

Since this photo was taken, the Dissel house was destroyed. Photo courtesy of Washington State Archives–Puget Sound Regional Branch.

a paint company. Records show that in 1917 he bought a house in Madison Park that had been built in 1906, and that he and Anna had three children—Albert, Jr., Marie, and Dorothy.

While the family lived on 39th Avenue North, Annette and two more boys, J. Kelton and Charles, were born. When they were of school age, all six of the Dissel children went to McGilvra School. Marie Dissel, born in 1912, went on to Broadway High School. Marie married Bus Hadfield, a McGilvra schoolmate, and lives in Madison Park to this day.

Long after the Dissels left their house, it was bought by Carl Bricken, who in 1943 became the Director and Conductor of the Seattle Symphony Orchestra. Bricken was born in Shelbyville, Kentucky, in 1898. He was educated at the Phillips Academy, Andover, Massachusetts, and graduated from Yale University in 1922. While there, Bricken was the leader of the college orchestra and conductor of the Yale Glee Club. After five years of studying composition and piano in New York and Europe, he married Dorothy Moran of Mendham, New Jersey. The Brickens had two children, Anne and Alexander "Sandy." Bricken was active in the fields of symphonic, choral, operatic, and chamber music as a composer, teacher, concert pianist, and conductor.

THE BURLINGAME HOUSE AND THE PRATT REMODEL BY GOWEN

Isaac Burlingame was granted a permit late in 1912 to build on the property he had owned for 6 years. This property was also the beneficiary of the 1908 document vacating this block of 42nd Avenue North. A widower and foreman at Alvord Automatic Machine Company, Burlingame purchased the lot from J. J. McGilvra's wife and children. According to the building permit, Burlingame's intention was to build a one-and-a half-story residence, at a cost of $1,600. By the time Burlingame completed his house, it faced the Lake and was on a parcel of waterfront property.

The Burlingame house has been altered since the photo was taken. Photo courtesy of Washington State Archives–Puget Sound Regional Branch.

The subsequent resident of the house was Dudley Pratt, born of American parents living in Paris in 1897. Dudley's father was a sculptor of considerable renown in Boston. The younger Pratt attended Yale University for two years, then left to join the Army when the United States became involved in World War I. Pratt returned to Boston and studied at the Museum School of Fine Arts, where he was awarded a generous scholarship. Pratt and his wife, Virginia Claflin, came to Seattle in 1926, and he joined the faculty at the University of Washington. Soon thereafter, they bought the Burlingame house and undertook an extensive remodeling project to accommodate their growing family. The Pratt children were Janna, Matthew, Susan, and "Tuckie." Lexie Spafford Robbins remembers visiting the Pratt home, where modeling clay was available for play.[18]

Two points of interest in the house are, first, the windowed room shown at the left of the front door, Pratt's studio, where he had space and light for his sculpting; and, second, that the house now faces west instead of east. By 1926, the house no longer stood on the shore of Lake Washington because of the lowering of the lake, and

Lancelot Edward Gowen was commissioned to draw plans for the remodel of their Madison Park home.

Chronicling Gowen's life, Jeffrey Karl Ochsner wrote that Lance was born in Seattle in 1894 and received his undergraduate degree in

architecture from the University of California at Berkeley in 1916. Following years as an Army infantry officer in World War I, he earned the M.A. in Architecture from U.C. Berkeley in 1921 and then studied at Ecole des Beaux Arts.[19]

The Pratt house has been altered. Photo courtesy of Bob Peterson.

Several years of study and travel culminated with Gowen's appointment as an instructor in the Department of Architecture at the University of Washington in 1924, and as an assistant professor the next year. It is fair to assume that Gowen and Pratt, as colleagues and just three years apart in age, would have been compatible for the remodeling project.

THE TIBBILS HOUSEBOAT

In 1918, a 1,064-square-foot, one-bedroom, one-bath, houseboat was built by the Lake. It was typical of many such homes in Madison Park, ever since John J. McGilvra's early plan for small lots with summer cottages. Although a few have survived with creative remodeling, many more have given way to larger homes that more comfortably accommodate families.

Hamilton and Alida Tibbils moved this houseboat, in 1933, from the lake to a lot one block west and placed it on pier blocks. This also presented them the opportunity to build an attached garage. A city

The Tibbils house was later destroyed. Photo courtesy of Washington State Archives–Puget Sound Regional Branch.

directory identifies Tibbils as the owner of Pine Street Super Service. His wife, who was born in Finland, was never without a dog and spent many hours in her garden.

THE TOURTELLOTTES' HOUSE

An article in the Seattle Times described the house on Hillside Drive as starting out as a little house in 1923, and then growing with the addition of the "big living room with the biggest window you have ever seen."[20] The ceiling does, indeed, reach to 12 feet in the fir-paneled room with a brick fireplace. The wooden house sits high on the steep lot, with the three-car garage and carriage house below at street level.

The original owners were Janet P. and Neal E. Tourtellotte. Neal, son of Della and John E. Tourtellotte, was born in Boise, Idaho, in 1894. By the time he was 21, John had already worked 4 years in construction and had some architectural drawing experience. He arrived in Idaho just 2 months after statehood, and by the time Neal was born, had decided to concentrate on design.

Early in the twentieth century, John formed an architectural firm with an employee, Charles Hummell, who had trained formally in his native Germany. The two men designed many homes, businesses, and churches across southern Idaho and southeastern Oregon. In addition to University of Idaho campus buildings, Tourtellotte and Hummell won the competition to design the Capitol building in Boise. His son Neal attended the Philips Exeter Academy in Exeter, New Hampshire, for prep school, and the Massachusetts Institute of Technology for his college education. Quoting from one of Neal's letters home, when he was serving overseas as a captain in the Army in World War I: "The Cathedral was a composite study in English architecture. Some of my classroom knowledge, gained in 'Architectural History,' was finally of use!"[21] For many years Neal was president of the Tourtellotte–Bradley Corporation, building specialties contractors. He also served as Director of the Northwest Regional Office of the Small Business Administration.

Janet and Neal worked closely with contractor Edward H. Noyes. She commented, "We love our home. It epitomizes the Northwest to us."[22]

The Tourtellotte house was subsequently altered. Photo courtesy of Washington State Archives–Puget Sound Regional Branch.

The Emerson house has been altered. Photo courtesy of Washington State Archives–Puget Sound Regional Branch.

THE EMERSON HOUSE AND ARCHITECT CHARLES STANLEY

In the next few years, from 1925 to 1927, 39th Avenue North, between Lee Street and Hillside Drive, developed from north to south. In 1925, Ralph G. Emerson and his wife, Florence L., were the original owners of a house described as five rooms on one floor, with an attic and a full basement. Features were hardwood floors and a brick fireplace. The house had a shingle exterior and a shake roof.

Emerson was born in Bangor, Maine, in 1892. When he was 20 years old, he moved to Spokane and attended Whitman College for 2 years. He then studied Business Administration at the University of Pittsburgh. During World War I he was a 2nd Lieutenant in the Army Tank Corps serving in France. The Emersons had two daughters.

On January 1, 1930, Emerson became the second general manager of the Broadmoor Golf Club. He served in this capacity for 2 years and then worked for the City of Seattle in the Purchasing Department for 22 years, until his retirement in 1955.

Records show that J. Charles Stanley was the architect of Emerson's house.[23] A city directory indicates that Stanley was associated with another architect, Earl A. Roberts, while Stanley was designing this house. The Emersons sold the house in 1937, and the new owners commissioned William Bain, Sr. to finish the second floor. Plans survive showing that they added three bedrooms and two baths to what had been the attic.[24]

THE TUDOR-STYLE CLISE HOUSE AND ARCHITECT HENRY BITTMAN

On 39th North in 1925, Charles Francis and Rosalind Hammer Clise commissioned Henry W. Bittman to design their home. Born in Seattle in 1890, Charles was the youngest child of Anna Herr and James William Clise. He graduated from Broadway High School and Yale University and followed in his father's footsteps as a second-generation community leader. Chairman of the Board of Clise and Cumins, Inc., and president of Securities Mortgage Company, he is known for

The Clise house was altered after the photo was taken. Photo courtesy of Washington State Archives–Puget Sound Regional Branch.

recognizing the long-term growth opportunities in Seattle's Denny Regrade. Charles and Rosalind had four children—Al, Jocelyn, Sylvia, and Charles, Jr.[25]

Architect of the Clise House, Henry Bittman, was born in Greenpoint, New York, in 1882. He studied engineering at Cooper Union and came to Seattle in 1906. According to Caterina Provost, by 1908 he had his own structural engineering practice, specializing in the design of structural steel skeletons for Seattle's new buildings.[26] The Tudor house Bittman built in 1914–15 for himself and his wife was one of his few residential designs. We might safely assume that by 1925 the Clises had seen and admired this Tudor home and asked Bittman to draw plans for their two-and-a-half-story home in Madison Park. The landscape design of the 180 x 130 square-foot property, complementing the house, was by Otto E. Holmdahl.

THE McWHIRTERS' STUCCO HOME
AND ARCHITECT EDWIN IVEY

A third home was built in 1925 on 39th Avenue North. The original owners of this stately stucco house were Elise Farrell and Earl Jack McWhirter. Jack was born in Chattanooga, Tennessee, in 1891, the youngest of four children. When he was 12, the family moved to Seattle, where he attended public schools. He later studied chemistry at Northern Pacific College in Portland.

While stationed in Alaska during World War I, Jack met the adventuresome Elise. She was from Ansonia, Connecticut, where her family owned the Farrell–Birmingham Company. The two were married in 1919. McWhirter owned the E. J. McWhirter Drug Company and then was president of the Tru-Bristle Brush Company in Ballard.

Both Jack and Elise were avid equestrians, and Jack played polo. They used the Arboretum stables and trails regularly, and ultimately bought property in Redmond, where they retired to raise horses. Today that property is known as Farrell–McWhirter Park, the couple's gift to the city of Redmond.

The McWhirter house has been altered. Photo courtesy of Washington State Archives–Puget Sound Regional Branch.

Six years after their marriage, they commissioned Edwin J. Ivey to design their Madison Park home. Jeffrey Karl Ochsner recorded that Ivey was born in Seattle in 1883. He earned a degree in architecture from the University of Pennsylvania in 1910 and, following graduation, returned to Seattle. Ivey moved from partnerships to private practice by 1922, remaining so until his accidental death in 1940.[27]

THE CAPE COD HAIGHT HOUSE AND ARCHITECT ARTHUR LOVELESS

The house at the corner of 39th Avenue North and Hillside Drive was built in 1926. It has been called a Cape Cod with one-and-a-half stories and a basement. The house has a shingle exterior and roof, with a rock wall toward the street and a flagstone terrace in the back. Interior features include three fireplaces, cedar beams, bookcases, and paneling.

Original owner James Augustus Haight, Jr. was born in Jamestown, North Dakota, in 1888. His father was the Olympia attorney with whom Mark Reed studied law in 1892. The Haight family moved to Seattle when James, Jr. was 16 years old. He attended public school, and then St. Paul's in Concord, New Hampshire.

James, Jr., graduated from Yale in 1911 and the University of Washington Law School, before enlisting as a duty sergeant in World War I. In 1920, he married Gertrude Boland in Grass Lake, Michigan. He practiced law with his father and brother in Seattle. In 1922, the Haights welcomed James III to their family.

The Haights commissioned Arthur Lamont Loveless to design their house. In Thomas Veith's account, Loveless was born in Big Rapids, Michigan, in 1873. At age 18, he moved to Manistee, Michigan, where he worked as a bookkeeper and at a bank. He was accepted in the architecture program at Columbia University in 1902. Loveless was forced to seek employment before completing his studies.[28]

Loveless came to Seattle around 1907 at the age of 27 and was involved primarily with houses and small commercial projects. The Loveless house was essentially an English Country house modified to fit a relatively dense suburban environment. Its placement between the street and a dramatic view is typical of Loveless's mature work, according to author Veith. The receiving rooms and most of the bedrooms are oriented to the view.

Subsequent to this photo, the Haight house was moved. Photo courtesy of Washington State Archives–Puget Sound Regional Branch.

New owners in the 1940s transformed the gardens of the Haight house. First there was a WWII Victory Garden, one of the 20 million planted throughout the country. Then, in the 1950s, Noble Hoggson designed a large rockery and a rose bed, and the vegetable garden became a competition-croquet lawn. In the 1960s, the Kubota family cleared blackberries and morning glory from the ravine, and 89-year-old Fujitaro created a Japanese garden with significant rocks, a series of pools, and a bridge.

Arthur Loveless and Edwin Ivey, considered the leading Seattle residential architects of the 1920s, designed these two houses for the McWhirter and Haight families, standing next door to each other on 39th Avenue North.

THE POWELLS' PROPERTY AND
RICHARDSON'S COTSWOLD DESIGN

George Powell wrote that his family began selling off parts of the 37th Avenue North property in the late 1920s.[29] The Dutch Colonial house was sold to James Irving and Ruth Clise Colwell in 1928. Ruth was the oldest child of Anna and James Clise. John and Elizabeth Powell were most likely ready to downsize, as their three older children had married and only the two younger boys were at home, when they were not away at school. They commissioned Paul David Richardson to design a Cotswold-style house on the northwest corner of the property.

Richardson, Thomas Veith wrote, was born in Smithsberg, Maryland, in 1888, and came to Seattle with his parents when he was very young.[30] He grew up in Seattle and attended Broadway High School. Following a brief architectural apprenticeship in 1910, he joined the representative of a New York firm hired by the Metropolitan Building Company to prepare a plan for development of the University's Metropolitan Tract. One might well assume that John Powell had done business with and admired the firm, in Powell's capacity as a University of Washington Regent.

In 1924, Richardson most likely was an associate on all of the

The Powell house was altered after the photo was taken. Photo courtesy of Washington State Archives–Puget Sound Regional Branch.

firm's drawings, including several additions and modifications to Children's Orthopedic Hospital, on whose Board of Trustees Elizabeth Powell served. Although primarily known as designers of commercial structures and churches, the members of the firm did complete some residential commissions.

Dorothy Cabot Best spent several years looking for just the right house. One day in 1936, she and an agent came upon the Powells' Cotswold house. The agent was dispatched to the door and shown in, where she told Elizabeth that Mrs. Best would like to buy her home. Elizabeth responded, "Well, why not?"[31] She had stayed on in this house for 6 years following the death of her husband, John.

Elizabeth then moved to the Gainsborough Apartments on First Hill, but she wanted to be back in Madison Park. William Bain, Sr. designed the one-story house for her early in 1941. In 1942, Elizabeth Powell, at age 76, moved into her new house in Madison Park—a home that allowed her to live independently until her last illness at age 80.

The houses profiled here range in age from being built in 1893 to 1951. They also range in size and in style. The houses speak to the eclectic nature of Madison Park and its residents. I am reminded of a grandchild asking, "What is a neighborhood?" I have introduced you to mine.

This Powell house was altered. Photo courtesy of Washington State Archives–Puget Sound Regional Branch.

A BRIEF HISTORY

COASTAL INDIAN CULTURES were firmly established in the Puget Sound area 2,000 years ago. Centuries later, adventurers from Europe and American cultures started exploring and claiming territories in the West. Adoption of the Declaration of Independence by the Continental Congress on July 4, 1776, is of primary significance. That same year, meeting in September, the second Continental Congress replaced the name "United Colonies" with "United States." The king of England was George III, and a full 7 years later, following the Revolutionary War, the British recognized the United States of America at the Treaty of Paris on September 4, 1783.

The year 1789 found General George Washington as the first President of the United States and Thomas Jefferson serving as his Secretary of State for the fledgling nation of 4,000,000 people. The next year, Congress moved from New York to Philadelphia.

Three thousand miles away on the same continent, an Indian boy named Sealth was just 3 years old. Born on what would later be called Blake Island in central Puget Sound, his father was chief of the Suquamish ("Outside") tribe and his mother, the chief's daughter of the Duwamish ("People of the Inside").

EUROPEAN SEA VOYAGES TO THE NORTHWEST

Early European sailing parties to the West Coast of North America included Spanish galleons looking for gold, Russian fur trappers seeking a more temperate climate, and English captains on voyages of discovery on behalf of the Crown. In the spring of 1792, exactly 300 years after Columbus came ashore in the Caribbean, Captain George Vancouver, a member of the British Royal Navy, arrived on the western shores of the new world. Another ship, flying the flag of the new United States, was captained by Robert Gray, who explored and named the "River of the West" for his vessel, the *Columbia*.

Vancouver and Gray met in late April, near what is known today as Cape Flattery, just south of the Strait of Juan de Fuca, and Vancouver's party continued north. Vancouver had logged two trips aboard Captain James Cook's ships on earlier voyages. When Vancouver set sail in 1791 as captain of HMS *Discovery* and came by way of the Cape of Good Hope in search of the Northwest Passage, he was accompanied by a second ship, the *Chatham*, with his good friend 2nd Lt. Peter Puget aboard. In the four-and-a-half years the two ships were away from England, they explored the coast from California to Alaska.

When Vancouver arrived at the Strait of Juan de Fuca with his crew of 180 men and looked south from the deck of the *Discovery* into Puget Sound, he was only 35 years old. He wrote in his journal, on May 8, 1792, "The round snowy mountain,…after my friend Rear Admiral Peter Rainier, I distinguish by the name of Mount Rainier." In the same year, on the opposite Coast, there was a ceremony for the laying of the cornerstone of the executive mansion, which later would become known as the White House.

The earlier Spanish ships had sailed north on inland waters from the Strait—as evidenced by the names of the islands they passed. Vancouver, however, chose to sail south. In addition to exploring and bestowing many place names, he and his men traveled all the way into the south Sound and maneuvered close to shore in smaller ships, keeping detailed logs and maps of the waters and the land. In 1798, Vancouver named this inland sea for Peter Puget—Puget Sound.

In 1800, the United States Congress met for the first time in Washington in the Capitol building still under construction. European and American politicians and merchants were anxious to lay claim to the western lands and the opportunities they offered. Plans for expansion and possession were limited by dependence on water. Until then, exploration, settlement, and commerce had followed navigable rivers or the open sea as the country's growth crept westward.

At the dawn of the nineteenth century, Thomas Jefferson was elected the third President of the United States. Even before his inauguration, he had asked another Virginia plantation owner, the son of a friend of his, to become his personal Secretary. That young man was Meriwether Lewis. Jefferson asked yet another fellow Virginian to be Secretary of State. This was James Madison, the principal writer of the Constitution and who, in 1809, succeeded Jefferson as the fourth President of the United States. When he died in 1836, at age 85, he was the last of the Founding Fathers.

President Thomas Jefferson was a man of letters, and in 1802 he and Meriwether Lewis studied the account of Britain's Alexander Mackenzie, who successfully completed a Canadian overland trek to the Pacific Ocean. It was clear to Jefferson that the United States must explore the land it had purchased from the French. He claimed Louisiana as "the high lands inclosing all the waters which run into the Mississippi or Missouri directly or indirectly." How extensive was this Missouri River and its western tributaries, and would this be the long-sought water route to the Pacific? Finding the answer to this question would allow the country to more clearly define the enormous new addition to the young republic. Jefferson also believed strongly that Britain was on the verge of claiming the northwest corner of the continent

Immediately upon the heels of his request to Congress for the millions of dollars to purchase the Louisiana Territory, Jefferson was granted a relatively modest $2,500 to finance an expedition that would follow the Missouri River, exploring the land and meeting the Indians who lived along the river. The President had a clear choice for the man to lead the expedition. He later wrote:

> "It was impossible to find a character who to a compleat science in botany, natural history, mineralogy & astronomy, joined the firmness of constitution & character, prudence, habits adapted to the woods, & a familiarity with the Indian manners & character, requisite for this undertaking. All the latter qualifications Capt. Lewis has."[1]

As Commander-in-Chief, and with the approval of Congress, the President turned to the War Department for men and monies to more adequately finance this project. The allowance enabled Lewis to recruit a second officer, another Virginian under whom he had served in the Chosen Rifle Company seven years earlier—William Clark. Clark was four years his senior, and the two men had known each other only six months. The five-page letter survives in which Lewis wrote about what transpired since they last met and, finally, on the fifth page, extended to Clark the invitation to join him on what would be named the Corps of Discovery.

THE JOURNEY OF LEWIS AND CLARK AND U.S. EXPANSION

Captains Lewis and Clark, with a team of 31 skilled botanists, zoologists, and survivalists, set out in 1804 upon their overland trip, which would include a winter encampment and arrival at the Pacific Ocean 18 months after their departure from St. Louis. This trek was arguably the single most important undertaking in the opening of the western United States to settlement.

1. Stephen Ambrose, *Undaunted Courage* (New York: Simon & Schuster, 1996) p.76.

In the continued struggle to define its boundaries with European nations, the United States waged the War of 1812 against Britain, which lasted until 1815. The Anglo–American Convention of 1818 established the 49th Parallel as the international boundary from the Lake of the Woods, Minnesota, to the Rocky Mountains. The United States and Britain postponed a decision on the boundary farther to the west and agreed to hold those lands in "joint occupancy" for 10 years. The United States had argued for a continuation of the 49th Parallel to the Pacific Coast, and Britain was just as determined to claim the territory north of the Columbia River, using the presence of the Hudson Bay Company as good reason for ownership.

In 1819, under the Adams–Onis Treaty, Article II, Spain ceded Florida to the United States "in full property and sovereignty." A more lengthy Article III stated that west of the Mississippi, the Spanish king, "his heirs, and successors, renounces all claim to said territories forever." The "said territories" were everything north of the 42nd Parallel, the California–Oregon border of today.

Congress appropriated funds to the Navy for a United States Exploring Expedition under the command of Charles Wilkes. The international trade in furs and whale products had become highly competitive, and this voyage set out in 1838 to circumnavigate the globe. Wilkes returned 4 years later with important documents, including a lengthy 1841 survey of the North American coast. The survey documented detailed observations in anthropology, geology, zoology, botany and, most important, cartography. Scholars determined that Elliott Bay was named for his midshipman, Samuel Elliott. In 1852, 11 years after his voyage, Wilkes said this Bay would become one of "the finest ports in the world."

Just 3 years after Wilkes's return to the East Coast, the first party of American settlers arrived in the Puget Sound region. They settled near Tumwater in 1845.

President James Knox Polk (1845–1849), who won his party's nomination by campaigning as the "candidate who stands for expansion," completed his term by leading the country in the acquisition of a million square miles of new territory. The Anglo–American Treaty of 1818 and "joint occupancy" of western territories became a campaign issue with Polk's battle cry of "Fifty-four Forty or Fight"—referring to the northern latitudinal line of the geographic area earmarked for acquisition. The United States had grown by one third in landmass and included Texas, Oregon, and California. Opportunities for moving West became much more inviting for adventuresome settlers, who were now under the protection of the United States.

The Treaty of Oregon, written in 1846, determined once and for all that the northern boundary of the United States would be the 49th Parallel. All of this western land was to be a part of the public domain with title vested in the federal government and "disposition thereof would be in accordance with statutory enactment." Ambiguity prevailed, however, as to the boundary as it weaved its way off the coast, through the San Juan Islands and south around Vancouver Island.

It took the Pig War in 1859, on San Juan Island, to begin to resolve the matter. The Pig War was so named because an American settler shot and killed a British Hudson's Bay Company pig found rooting for potatoes in his garden. After more than 10 years of armed hostility between the two nations' Island camps, the pig was the only fatality. Later still, with Kaiser Wilhelm of Prussia mediating, what would be Anglo and what would be American was finally determined.

The War with Mexico was fought in the Southwest from 1846–1848. Until that time, the United States and Mexico were the two largest independent countries in North America. When Texas was admitted to the Union in 1845, as the fifteenth state, Mexico decided to cross the Rio Grande and fight to hold that valuable land along its northern border.

The Seneca Falls Convention in New York State in 1848 marked the initiation of women's rights. Elizabeth Cady Stanton and Lucretia Mott wrote "The Declaration of Rights and Sentiments," modeled after Thomas Jefferson's words 75 years earlier. The ladies announced that the meeting would be in the Wesleyan Chapel, and thus began the Women's Suffrage Movement.

SETTLING THE OREGON TERRITORY

Also in 1848, and with the assistance of maps from the Wilkes Expedition, the Oregon Territory was named and would include the area we know today as Oregon, Washington, Idaho, and western Montana. While he was in the northwestern corner of the Territory, Isaac Neff Ebey, age 30, passed a large freshwater lake and named it Geneva. He kept moving north and settled on Whidbey Island, then sent for his wife and children to join him. Six years later, Asa Shinn Mercer honored the nation's first president by renaming the lake with the 50-mile shoreline after the nation's first president, and so it became Lake Washington.

In California, 1849 marked the year of impetus for many thousands to rush west—not for land, but for gold. General John A. Sutter's sawmill, about 150 miles east of San Francisco at the convergence of the American and Sacramento Rivers, became the destination for miners from around the world. By and large, this was a migration of men, who made the 6- to 9-month trip overland or by sea to stake their claims, make their fortunes, then return home to their families. California, newly wrested from Mexico and not yet a state until 1850, became the promised land for the hopeful, who could not have imagined the hardships of the travel and the misery of frontier living.

Initially the settled land could be owned by the grantee only after 4 years of settlement. At such time, he would receive a patent for his land "as the free gift of a generous nation." Many settlers suffered hardship at having to wait so long for ownership, so the donation act was amended to read that after 2 years, a claimant might purchase his land for $1.25 per acre.

Men still greatly outnumbered women in the Territory, enhancing the occasion of many child brides. An "old maid" was an unmarried female 12 years or older. Money, in the form of cold, hard coin, was almost nonexistent in early territorial days. Title to land, permanent and indestructible, became essential in the creation of wealth. In Washington Territory alone, 290,000 acres were claimed during the 5-year window of opportunity between September 1850 and December 1855.

NOTES

INTRODUCTION

1. Denny, Emily Inez, *Blazing the Way* (Seattle: Rainier Printing Company, Inc., 1909), p31

2. Arthur A. Denny.

CHAPTER 1: THE EARLY DAYS

1. Ezra Meeker, in *Washington Territory West of the Cascade Mountains* (Olympia, WA: Transcript Office, 1870).

2. Olive Baker McDougall, *Where the Tiger Lilies Grew*, 2002, unpublished, housed in McGilvra School library.

3. Robert E. Ficken, *Lumber and Politics* (Seattle: University of Washington Press, 1979), p. 12.

4. Andrew Price, Jr., *Port Blakely* (Seattle: Port Blakely Books, 1989), p. 92.

5. Ficken, *Lumber and Politics*, p. 14.

6. Ficken, *Lumber and Politics*, p. 8.

7. Ficken, *Lumber and Politics*, p. 9.

8. Ficken, *Lumber and Politics*, p. 19.

9. James R. Warren, *A Centennial History of the Seattle Tennis Club* (Bellevue: Vernon Publication, 1990).

10. George Van Tuyl Powell, *A Family History*, 1993, unpublished.

11. Jeffrey Karl Ochsner and Dennis Alan Anderson, *Distant Corners: Seattle Architects and the Legacy of H. H. Richardson.* Seattle and London: Univer-

sity of Washington Press, 2003), p. 207.

12. George Powell, in *A Family History*.

13. Jacqueline Lawson and Jim Yarbrough, coordinators, *Washington State ROOTS, Twentieth Anniversary Celebration Souvenir Booklet* (Seattle: Jacqueline Lawson, 1992).

14. Paul Dorpat, *Seattle Now and Then* (Seattle: Tartu Publications, 1984).

15. Richard Berner, *Seattle 1900–1920* (Seattle: Charles Press, 1991), p. 129.

16. James R. Warren, *Where Mountains Meet the Sea* (Northridge, CA: Windsor Publications Inc., 1986).

17. Henry Schmitz, *The Long Road Traveled* (Seattle: Arboretum Foundation, 1973).

18. Donald N. Sherwood, *Interpretive Essays of the Histories of Seattle's Parks and Playgrounds* (Seattle: University of Washington Libraries, Special Collections, 1980).

19. Quote from www.historylink.org

20. In Powell's *A Family History*.

21. Janet Powell Tourtellotte, in her unpublished "Letter to Two Nieces.", 1967

22. In Berner's *Seattle 1900–1920*, pp. 89, 137.

23. Emilie Bloch Schwabacher, *A Place for the Children* (Seattle: Children's Hospital and Medical Center, 1992).

24. In Powell's *A Family History*.

25. Jacqueline B. Williams, *The Hill With a Future* (Seattle: CPK Ink, 2001).

26. Unpublished memoir by Olive Baker McDougall.

27. In Berner's *Seattle 1900–1920*, p. 60.

28. In Berner's *Seattle 1900–1920*, p. 60.

29. Barbara H. Stenson, *A Bridge Over Time* (Seattle: Church of the Epiphany, 1997), p. 7.

CHAPTER 2: A NEW CENTURY

1. Janet Powell Tourtellotte, "Letter to Two Nieces," unpublished.

2. George Van Tuyl Powell, *A Family History*, 1993, unpublished.

3. *Washington Educational Journal*, March 1937.

4. *The Seattle Times*, March 11, 1930.

5. Donald N. Sherwood, *Interpretive Essays of the Histories of Seattle's Parks and Playgrounds* (Seattle: University of Washington Libraries, Special Collections, 1980).

6. Emilie Schwabacher, *A Place for the Children* (Seattle: Children's Hospital and Medical Center, 1992). As a side note, Schwabacher's husband (Morton's family) owned the hardware store that outfitted miners on their way to the Klondike in 1897.

7. Author's interviews with Bruce Shorts, September, 2000.

8. Olive Baker McDougall, *Where the Tiger Lilies Grew*, 2002, unpublished, housed in McGilvra School Library.

9. Forrest B. Richardson, *An Historical Perspective* (Seattle: Superior Publishing Company, 1983).

10. Jeff Mingay, "Architect Ahead of His Time." *Links magazine*, January/February 2002.

11. Almira Bailey, article in the *Seattle Post–Intelligencer*, August 22, 1927.

12. Grant Hildebrand wrote the essay "John Graham, Sr." for the book *Shaping Seattle Architecture*, edited by Jeffrey Karl Ochsner (Seattle: University of Washington Press, 1994).

13. Author's interview with Augusta Davis McClain.

14. David Rash wrote the essay "Schack, Young and Myers" for the book *Shaping Seattle Architecture* (Seattle: University of Washington Press, 1994).

15. Richard Berner, *Seattle 1900–1920* (Seattle: Charles Press, 1991), p. 54.

16. Berner, p. 126.

17. Robert E. Ficken, *Lumber and Politics* (Seattle: University of Washington Press, 1979), p. 23.

18. Ficken's *Lumber and Politics*, p. 9.

19. Robert Spector, *Family Trees: Simpson's Centennial Story* (Bellevue, WA: Documentary Book Publishers Corporation, 1990), p. 46.

20. In Berner's book, *Seattle 1900–1920*, p. 129.

21. In Sherwood's *Interpretive Essays*.

22. In Berner's *Seattle 1900–1920*, p. 77.

23. In Powell's *A Family History*.

24. Olive Baker McDougall's *Where the Tiger Lilies Grew*.

25. Jim Brown, *Hubbard: The Forgotten Boeing Aviator* (Vancouver, British Columbia.: Peanut Butter Publishing, 1996).

26. Excerpts from letters Neal Tourtellotte sent home to his family.

27. Excerpts from unpublished Log in the Museum of Flight collection, Seattle.

28. Letter from Mary Morrison Jaynes to Ethel Morrison Mendelson, December 25, 1923.

29. Robert Spector, "Eddie Bauer: The Man Behind the Name," *Pacific Northwest Magazine,*Vol. 17, No. 4, May 1983.

20. Spector's article.

CHAPTER 3: PRE-WAR AND THE WAR YEARS

1. Robert Spector, *Family Trees: Simpson's Centennial Story* (Bellevue, WA: Documentary Book Publishers Corporation, 1990), p. 50.

2. Thomas Veith wrote the essay on Arthur L. Loveless for *Shaping Seattle Architecture* (Seattle: University of Washington Press, 1994).

3. As reported on www.historylink.org by Paula Becker and Greg Lange.

4. Author's 2003 interview with Taylor Scott, who grew up in Madison Park and graduated from McGilvra School.

5. Author's 2003 interview with Bernie and Mitzi Hagan, she a life-long resident of Madison Park

6. James M. Burns, *The Lion and The Fox* (New York: Harcourt, 1956).

7. Jack and Dorothy Yamaguchi, *This Was Minidoka* (Nagaoka, Japan: Nagai Printing Company, Ltd., 1989; and Tacoma: Pollard Printing Group, Inc., 1992).

8. James R Warren, *The War Years: A Chronicle of Washington State in World War II* (Seattle: History Ink, 2000).

9. A copy of the original document, dated January 29, 1942, and signed by Powell, exists in a private collection.

10. Author's interviews with Bruce Shorts in September 2000.

11. Colonel Charles Pye "Bert" Burnett, Jr., was born August, 14, 1904, in Seattle, graduated from Broadway High School and University of Washington undergraduate and law schools. Died July 26, 1944, on Florida Island, while flying as an emissary for General George C. Marshall to meet with General Douglas MacArthur in Australia.

12. Bruce Shorts interviews, September 2000.

13. Bruce Shorts interviews, September 2000.

14. B-17 bomber jingle found on the Web.

15. Author's interviews with James K. Marshall, 2002. He was born in Seattle in 1926 and moved to Madison Park in 1958.

16. Author's interviews in 2002 with Douglas A. Fields, who grew up in Madison Park

17. Author's interviews in 2003 with Mitzi Balkema Hagan, a life-long resident of Madison Park

18. Author's interviews with Bernie and Mitzi Hagan, 2003.

19. Quotes by Bill Reed in *Family Trees*, by Robert Spector, p. 80.

20. In George Powell's *A Family History*.

21. John Rupp, in an unpublished paper titled, "The North Pacific Balloon Caper," January 1991. Rupp was born in Seattle in 1913, graduated from Garfield High School, and from the University of Washington as an undergraduate in 1934 and law in 1937.

22. Hagan interviews, 2003.

23. Author's interview with Doug Fields, 2003. Fields, a grandson of Seattle pioneer Thomas Eustus "Tess" MacLachlan, moved to Madison Park in 1939, graduating from McGilvra, Garfield, and the University of Washington.

24. A copy was provided, by Harvard University Archives, of Jay Morrison's "Application for a Scholarship," dated January 20, 1908.

CHAPTER 4: MADISON PARK BUSINESSES

1. Olive Baker McDougall, *Where the Tiger Lilies Grew*, 2002, unpublished, housed in McGilvra School library.

2. George Van Tuyl Powell, *A Family History*, 1993, unpublished.

3. Author's interviews in 2002 with Doug Fields, who grew up in Madison Park.

4. Author's interview in 2003 with Mitzi Hagan, life-long resident of Madison Park.

5. Marilyn Warner, "In Madison Park, it's an institution," in the Pictorial section, *The Seattle Times*, October 7, 1973.

6. Author's interviews with Bill Buchan, 2003.

7. "A Conversation with Bill Buchan," at www.mycstar.org/stardust/buchan-boats_files/buchanboats.htm

8. Duane A. Dietz wrote the essay "William J. Bain, Sr." for *Shaping Seattle Architecture*, edited by Jeffery Karl Ochsner (Seattle: University of Washington Press, 1994).

9. In *Building Together*, by William J. and Mildred C. Bain (Seattle: Beckett

Publishing Company, 1991).

10. Bain and Bain, *Building Together.*

11. Dietz. See Note 8.

12. An interview with Paul Thiry by Meredith Clausen, Smithsonian Archives of American Art, 1983. http://artarchives.si.edu/oralhist/thiry83.htm

13. Meredith L. Clausen wrote the essay "Paul Thiry" for *Shaping Seattle Architecture.*

14. Grant Hildebrand wrote the essay "John Graham, Sr." for *Shaping Seattle Architecture.*

15. Bert Croshaw's interview printed in *Madison Park Times, Residents' Guide,* January 1994.

16. Bert Croshaw's *A Personal History,* 1980, unpublished; courtesy of Roger Croshaw.

17. Interview in Seattle with Kenneth J. Lindley recorded in *University Federal Savings and Loan Association Gazette,* Vol. 1, No. 1, 1973.

18. Interview by Don Plumlee, pharmacist and associate of Ken Lindley, who saw Ken as his mentor.

19. Author's interviews with Lola McKee in 2000.

20. Author's interview with Susan Trimble Svenson.

21. Author's interview with Hannahbeth Stern, 2003.

22. Author's interviews with Art Ackerman, 2003.

CHAPTER 5: MADISON PARK HOMES

1. Olive Baker McDougall, *Where the Tiger Lilies Grew,* 2002, unpublished, housed in McGilvra Library.

2. Aubrey Haines, *Mountain Fever* (Seattle: University of Washington Press, 1999).

3. In *Mountaineer Bulletin Notes,* November 11, 1916.

4. George Powell, in *A Family History,* unpublished, 1993.

5. Henry Matthews wrote the essay "Kirtland K. Cutter" for *Shaping Seattle Architecture* (Seattle: University of Washington Press, 1994).

6. Emilie Schwabacher, *A Place for the Children* (Seattle: Children's Hospital and Medical Center, 1992).

7. *Building Together,* by William J. and Mildred C. Bain (Seattle: Beckett Pub-

lishing Company, 1991).

8. Duane E. Dietz wrote the essay "William J. Bain, Jr." for *Shaping Seattle Architecture.*

9. Frank Calvert, editor, *Homes and Gardens of the Pacific Coast* (Beaux Arts Village, Lake Washington: Beaux Arts Society Publishers, 1913).

10. From a letter by Claire Hyde Jones, 1968, unpublished.

11. From a later letter by Claire Hyde Jones, 1968, unpublished.

12. Article titled "Dinner and Music, Charming Entertainment Given by Mr.and Mrs. Samuel Hyde," further information unavailable.

13. From the letter by Claire Hyde Jones; see Note 11.

14. David A. Rash and Dennis A. Anderson wrote the essay "Bebb & Mendel" for *Shaping Seattle Architecture.*

15. Rash and Anderson essay, "Bebb & Mendel" in *Shaping Seattle Architecture.*

16. An article by Dorothy Brant Brazier about the Hyde house, published in *The Seattle Times,* February 5, 1968.

17. From the letter by Claire Hyde Jones; see Note 11.

18. Author's interview in 2002 with Lexie Spafford Robbins, who grew up in Madison Park and graduated from McGilvra and Garfield schools.

19. Jeffrey Karl Ochsner, editor of *Shaping Seattle Architecture.*

20. Excerpted from "Leading Ladies of Seattle," *The Seattle Times,* January 17, 1937.

21. Excerpt from letter by Neal Tourtellotte to his family in 1917.

22. From "Leading Ladies of Seattle," *The Seattle Times,* January 17, 1937.

23. The source for this information is the Department of Construction and Land Use.

24. Plans by Naramore, Bain, Brady and Johanson.

25. *The Seattle Times,* July 7&8, 1961, B4.

26. Caterina Provost wrote the essay "Henry W. Bittman" for *Shaping Seattle Architecture.*

27. Jeffrey Karl Ochsner, *Shaping Seattle Architecture.*

28. Thomas Veith wrote the essay "Arthur L. Loveless" for *Shaping Seattle Architecture.*

29. George Powell, in *A Family History.*

30. Thomas Veith wrote the essay "Albertson, Wilson & Richardson" for *Shaping Seattle Architecture.*

31. Author's interview in 2003 with Pamela Best, daughter of Dorothy and Ivan Best, owners of Best's Apparel, purchased by Nordstrom's shoe store in 1963.

INFORMATION ON THE ORIGINAL HOMEOWNERS IN CHAPTER 5 WAS GAINED FROM THE FOLLOWING SOURCES:

1. Bricken, Carl: Capitol's "Who's Who For Washington"

2. Burlingame, Isaac: *Polk (Seattle) City Directories*

3. Clise, Charles F.: daughter Sylvia Duryee; *The Seattle Times*, July, 7&8, 1961, B4

4. Davis, C. Edwin: daughter Augusta McClain

5. Emerson, Ralph G.: *Polk (Seattle) City Directories*; Forrest B. Richardson, *An Historical Perspective* (Seattle: Superior Publ.,1983), p. 61; *The Seattle Times*, Dec. 4, 1966, B4

6. Haight, James A., Jr.: James A. Haight III; *Seattle & Environs*, Vol. 2, by C.H. Hanford (Chicago & Seattle: Pioneer Historical Publishing Co., 1924), pp. 563–564

7. Hyde, Samuel: papers from Nancy and Jeff Ewell; *Homes and Gardens of the Pacific Coast*, Vol.1, edited by Frank Calvert (Seattle: Beaux Arts Village, Lake Washington, 1913); *The Seattle Times*, May 22, 1944, B4

8. McWhirter, Earl Jack: *Seattle & Environs*, Vol. 3, by C.H. Hanford (Chicago & Seattle: Pioneer Historical Publishing Co., 1924), pp. 536–537; J. Vernon Williams

9. Powell, John H.: family journals, obituaries March 1930

10. Pratt, Dudley: daughter Tuckie Price

11. Spickard, Vernon W.: daughter-in-law Josephine Spickard; "A Place for the Children," by Emilie B. Schwabacher

12. Tibbels, Hamilton: *Polk (Seattle) City Directories*

13. Tourtellotte, Neal E.: family journal and letter; Emilie B. Schwabacher, "A Place for the Children"; *The Seattle Times*, Jan.17, 1937, and June 29, 1961, B4

14. Wright, George E.: Aubrey Haines, *Mountain Fever* (Seattle: University of Washington Press, 1999), pp.178, 240; *Seattle & Environs*, Vol. 2, by C. H. Hanford (Chicago & Seattle: Pioneer Historical Publishing Co., 1924), pp. 276–277; *Seattle Post Intelligencer*, Aug. 12, 1894.

BIBLIOGRAPHY

Ambrose, Stephen E. *Undaunted Courage: Meriwether Lewis, Thomas Jefferson and the Opening of the American West.* New York: Simon & Schuster, 1996.

Bagley, Clarence B. The History of Seattle from Its Earliest Settlement to the Present Time (3 vols). Chicago: S. J. Clarke, 1916.

Bain, William J., and Mildred C. *Building Together, A Memoir of Our Lives in Seattle.* Seattle: Beckett Publishing Company, 1991.

Berner, Richard C. *Seattle 1900–1920: From Boomtown, Urban Turbulence, to Restoration.* Seattle: Charles Press, 1991.

Brown, Jim. *Hubbard: The Forgotten Boeing Aviator.* Vancouver, British Columbia: Peanut Butter Publishing, 1996.

Burnham, Howard J. *For the Land's Sake!* Vancouver, WA: Oregon Historical Society and Clark County Title Company, 1952.

Burns, James M. *The Lion and The Fox.* New York: Harcourt, 1956.

Calvert, Frank, Editor. *Homes and Gardens of the Pacific Coast* (Vol. 1). Beaux Arts Village: Society Publishers, 1913.

Clausen, Meredith L. *Paul Thiry,* taped at the artist's home, transcribed and published by the Smithsonian Institution as a part of the Archives of American Art, September, 1983.

Dabney, Ellen Powell. Memorial. *Washington Educational Journal,* March 1937.

Denny, Emily Inez. *Blazing the Way.* Seattle: Rainier Printing Co., 1909.

Dorpat, Paul. "Now and Then" weekly columns in *The Seattle Times,* 2000–2004.

Dorpat, Paul, *Seattle, Now and Then, 1882–1984.* Seattle: Tartu Publications, 1984.

Ficken, Robert E. *Lumber and Politics: The Career of Mark E. Reed*. Seattle: University of Washington Press, 1979.

Haines, Aubrey. *Mountain Fever*. Seattle: University of Washington Press, 1999.

Hanford, C.H. *Seattle and Environs, 1852–1924*. Chicago & Seattle: Pioneer Historical Publishing Co., 1924.

Hilson, Stephen. *Exploring Puget Sound and British Columbia*. Seattle: Evergreen Pacific Publishing, Ltd., 1996.

Jackson, Donald, Editor. *Letters of the Lewis and Clark Expedition with Related Documents: 1783 – 1854, 2d edition* (Vol. 1). Urbana: University of Illinois Press, 1978.

Jaynes, Mary Morrison. Unpublished letter, December 25, 1923.

Kruckeberg, Arthur R. *The Natural History of Puget Sound Country*. Seattle: University of Washington Press, 1991.

Lawson, Jacqueline E.A., and Jim Yarbrough, coordinators. *Washington State ROOTS, Twentieth Anniversary Celebration Souvenir Booklet*. Seattle: Jacqueline Lawson, 1992.

Lehman, Richard Carl. "Revisiting the Park," *Madison Park Times*, April 2003.

Mac Donald, Howard E. *Seattle Post Intelligencer*, October 5, 1942, p. 1.

Madison Park Times, Residents' Guide, 1994.

McDougall, Olive Baker. *Where the Tiger Lilies Grew*. Unpublished manuscript, McGilvra School Library, 2000.

Meeker, Ezra. *Seventy Years of Progress in Washington*. Tacoma, WA: Allstrum Printing Co., 1921.

Meeker, Ezra. *Washington Territory West of the Cascade Mountains*. Olympia, WA: Transcript Office, 1870.

Mingay, Jeff. "Architect Ahead of His Time." *Links*, January/February 2002.

Morrison, Edward H. *Log - First Dawn to Dusk Flight, Los Angeles to Seattle*. Unpublished manuscript, 1923.

Ochsner, Jeffrey Karl, Editor. *Shaping Seattle Architecture: A Historical Guide to the Architects*. Seattle: University of Washington Press, 1994.

Ochsner, Jeffrey Karl, and Dennis Alan Anderson. *Distant Corners: Seattle Architects and the Legacy of H. H. Richardson*. Seattle & London: University of Washington Press, 2003.

Polk, Ralph Lane. *Polk (Seattle) City Directory*. Detroit: R. L. Polk Co., 1870.

Powell, George V. *A Family History*. Unpublished manuscript, 1993.

Price, Andrew, Jr. *Port Blakely: The Community Captain Renton Built*. Seattle:

Port Blakely Books, 1989.

Richardson, Forrest B. *An Historical Perspective.* Seattle: Superior Publishing Company, 1983.

Rochester, Junius. *The Last Electric Trolley.* Seattle: Tommie Press, 2002.

Rupp, John N. "The North Pacific Balloon Caper." Unpublished paper, January 1991.

Schmid, Calvin F. *Social Trends in Seattle* [University of Washington Studies in the Social Sciences, Vol. 14]. Seattle: University of Washington Press, 1944.

Schmitz, Henry. *The Long Road Travelled.* Seattle: Arboretum Foundation, 1973.

Schwabacher, Emilie B. *A Place for the Children: A Personal History of Children's Orthopedic Hospital and Medical Center.* Seattle: Children's Hospital and Medical Center, 1992.

The Seattle Times, October 5, 1942, p. 5.

Sherwood, Donald N. *Interpretive Essays of the Histories of Seattle's Parks and Playgrounds.* Unpublished, University of Washington Special Collections, 1980.

Spector, Robert. "Eddie Bauer: The Man Behind the Name," *Pacific Northwest Magazine,* Vol.17, No. 4, May 1983.

Spector, Robert. *Family Trees: Simpson's Centennial Story.* Bellevue, WA: Documentary Book Publishers Corp., 1990.

Stenson, Barbara H. *A Bridge Over Time: Seattle's Church of the Epiphany (Episcopal) 1907–1997.* Seattle: Church of the Epiphany, 1997.

Tourtellotte, Janet P. "Letter to Two Nieces." Unpublished, 1967.

Tourtellotte, Neal E. Unpublished letters, 1917–1918.

University Federal Savings and Loan Association *Gazette,* Vol. 1, No. 1, 1973.

Warren, James R. *A Centennial History of the Seattle Tennis Club.* Bellevue, WA: Vernon Publication Inc., 1990.

Warren, James R. *King County and Its Queen City: Seattle.* Woodland Hills, CA: Windsor Publications, Inc., 1981.

Warren, James R. *The War Years: A Chronicle of Washington State in World War II.* Seattle: History Ink, 2000.

Warren, James R. *Where Mountains Meet the Sea.* Northridge, CA: Windsor Publications, Inc., 1986.

Warren, James R., and William R. McCoy. *Highlights of Seattle's History.* Seattle: Historical Society of Seattle and King County, 1982.

Williams, Jacqueline B. *The Hill With a Future: Seattle's Capitol Hill 1900–1946.*

Seattle: CPK Ink, 2001.

Yamaguchi, Jack. *This Was Minidoka.* Nagaoka, Japan: Nagai Printing Co., Ltd., 1989.

ACKNOWLEDGMENTS

Carolyn Acheson – copyeditor

Richard C. Berner – author and historian

Sandra Blanton – librarian, McGilvra School

Linda Di Biase – librarian, Special Collections, University of Washington, Department of Architecture.

Al Doggett – photo restoration

Paul Dorpat – photographic historian

John Elliott – Systems Editor, *Seattle Daily Journal of Commerce*

Robert E. Ficken - author

Sharon Finn – librarian, McGilvra School

Dorothy Frick - photographer

Silja Griffin – General Manager, Seattle Tennis Club

Steve Hall – General Manager, Broadmoor Golf Club

Dan Hill – Golf professional, Broadmoor Golf Club

Kevin Hou – Administration Specialist, Department of Construction and Land Use

Greg Lange – research assistant, Washington State Archives, Puget Sound Regional Branch

Gary Luke – Vice President, Editorial Director, Sasquatch Books

Carolyn J. Marr – librarian, Museum of History and Industry

Bob McIntyre – historian, Seattle Mountaineers

Sandra Montgomery – permit technician, Department of Construction and Land Use

Jeffrey Karl Ochsner – Professor, University of Washington, Department of Architecture, and author

Perkins Studio – photographs

Andrew Price, Jr. – author

David A. Rash – architectural historian

Carla Rickerson – Head of Special
  Collections, University of Washington Library

Junius Rochester – author

Kate Rogers – editor

Eileen Ryan-Rojas – Alumni Director, Seattle Preparatory School

Karen Schober – book designer

Robert Spector – author

Phil Stairs – research assistant, Wash.
  State Archives, Puget Sound
  Regional Branch

Paul Talbert – Rainier Valley Historical Society

Eleanor Toews – archivist and
  records manager, Seattle Public
  Schools

Marilyn R. Warner - photographer

Dr. Gary A. Zimmerman – historian,
  Pioneer Association of the State of
  Washington

Carol Stigenwalt Allen
Carole Badgley
Nancy and Bill Bain
Jean and Charlie Barker
Pamela Best
Candy Wing BeVan
Gloria Bjornerud
Sally Clise Black
Robin Ryan Blanchett
Judi Donnan Boa
Eleanor Schwabacher Boren
Corie Stern Golub Borish
Helen Stevenson Brunn
Bill Buchan
Jim Callaghan
Peggy Sue Graham Carvalho–Maia
Mary Jane Jacobs Clark

Janine Severac Coburn
Candi Coe
Dr. Robert Coe
Stephanie Coen
Roseanne Stern Cohn
Sue Ann and Roger Croshaw
Vicky and Ray Downs
Sue Draper
Sylvia Clise Duryee
Sheila Pollard Dye
Betsy Hoak Edgerton
Nancy and Jeff Ewell
Doug Fields
Steve Frink
Laura Burnett Gowen
Dr. Charles Haberkern
Marie Dissel Hadfield
Roxanne Hadfield
Russell Hadfield
Bernie and Mitzi Hagan
Jim Haight III
Bill Hofius
Bill Hoppin
Katherine Colwell Howard
Virginia Vining Hughes
Jean English Jones
Jacqueline Lawson
Avonne Wilson Liebrant
Laura Ingham Lundgren
Dorthea and Jim Marshall
Augusta Davis McClain
Lola McKee
Linda Miller
Bob Mooney
Susan and Furman Moseley
Vicki Shorts Neumann
Ben Pelly
Nancy and Dudes Pelly
Lynn and Bob Peterson
Dr. Merle Pierce
Don Plumlee

Barbara Grace Powell
Molly Brown Pressey
Tuckie Pratt Price
Gary Reed
Ron Richardson
Lexie Spafford Robbins
Jan and Mac Rogers
Pamela Rolfe
Taylor Scott
Bruce Shorts
Susan Hawkes Spencer
Josephine McColl Spickard
Hannahbeth Spring Stern
Nancy and Fred Stoll

Susan Trimble Svenson
Linda Tallahan
Alice Wanamaker
Robert Denny Watt
Mary and Vern Williams
Fred Willis
Peggy Wilton
Rose Yamaguchi
Joan Powell Youngblood

INDEX

ABOUT THE AUTHOR

Jane Powell Thomas is the author of *Parenting Your Parents: How to Honor Quality of Life and Death*, published by Elfin Cove Press. She earned an undergraduate degree in English Literature from Smith College, and a master's degree in Psychology from Antioch University. Today, Jane is a busy mother of three children and grandmother of seven, and maintains a private practice as a Licensed Mental Health Counselor. In 1900 Jane's grandparents purchased and built on a homesite in Madison Park. Jane continues to live in Madison Park.